FIRST 50 SONGS

YOU SHOULD PLAY ON DRUMS

CONTENTS

Alive

Music by Stone Gossard
Lyric by Eddie Vedder

Intro
Moderately slow Rock ♩ = 76

Verse

"Son," she said... *Play 6 times*

Chorus

I'm, oh, I'm still a - live...

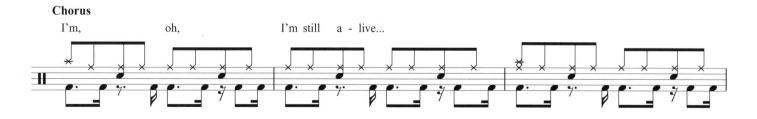

Verse

While she walks slow - ly...

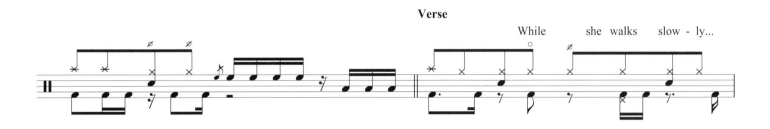

Chorus

I just stare...

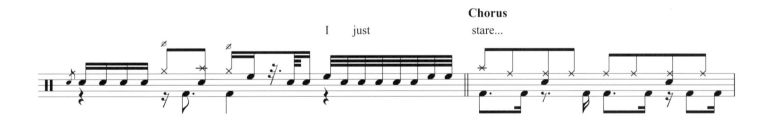

Bridge

"Is some-thing wrong?" she said...

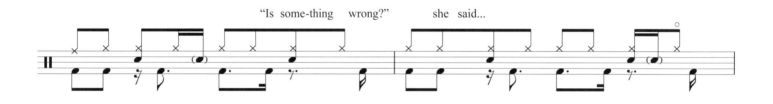

Chorus

I'm, oh, I'm still a - live...

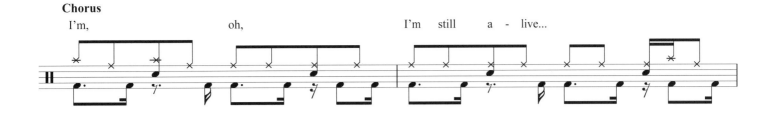

Guitar Solo

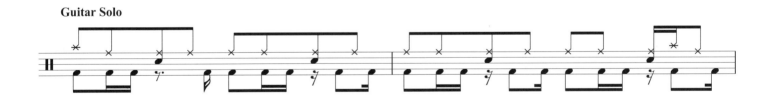

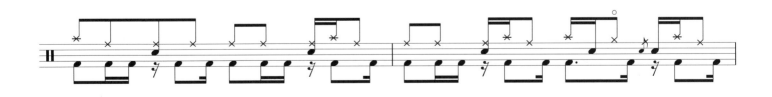

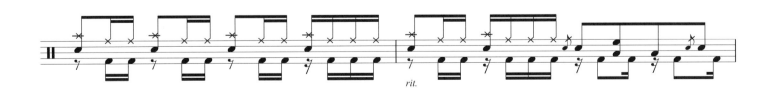

Free time

All Right Now

Words and Music by Andy Fraser and Paul Rodgers

Verse

I took her home to my

place...

Play 8 times

Chorus

All right now...

Guitar Solo

Play 3 times

Play 8 times

Play 10 times

Bridge

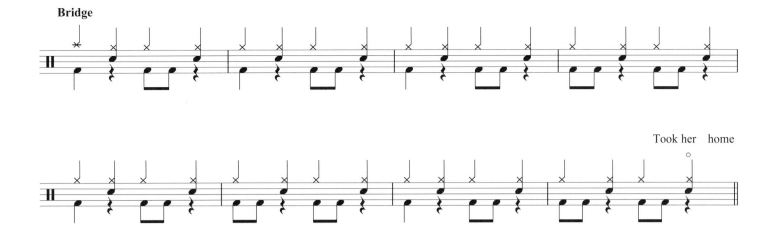

Took her   home

Verse

to   my   place...

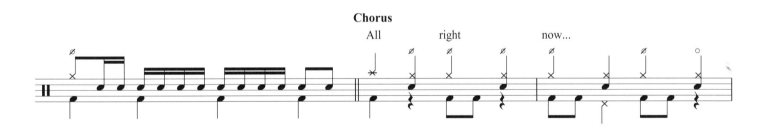

Chorus

All   right   now...

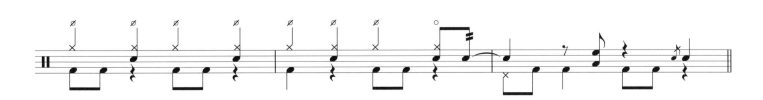

Outro-Chorus

All right   now...

Free time

rit.

Are You Gonna Go My Way

Words by Lenny Kravitz
Music by Lenny Kravitz and Craig Ross

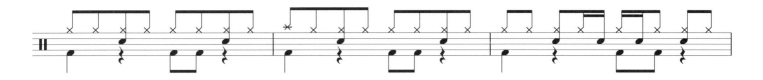

Interlude

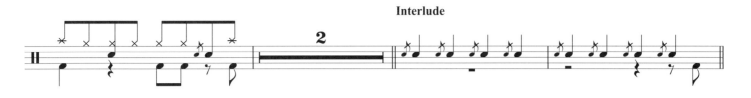

Guitar Solo

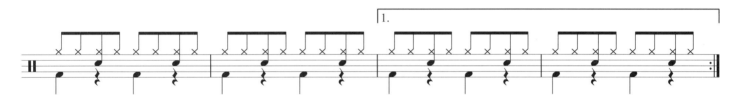

Chorus

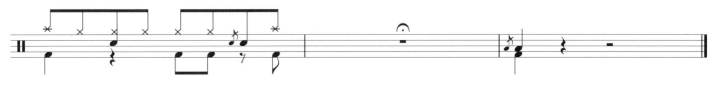

American Idiot

Words by Billie Joe
Music by Green Day

% Chorus

Wel-come to a   new   kind   of   ten - sion...

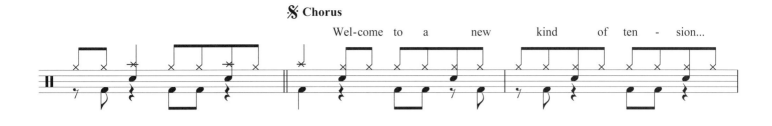

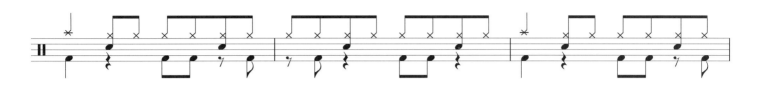

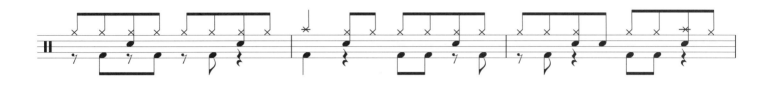

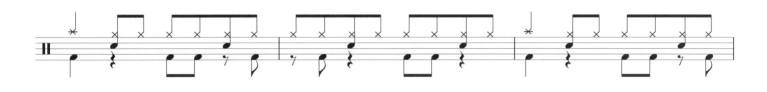

To Coda 2 ⊕

To Coda 1 ⊕

Verse

Well, may - be   I'm   the   fag - got   A - mer - i - ca...

D.S. al Coda 1

Coda 1

Interlude

Play 4 times

D.S. al Coda 2

...it's call - ing out   to id - i - ot A - mer - i - ca.

Coda 2

Outro

Beast of Burden

Words and Music by Mick Jagger and Keith Richards

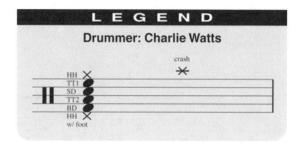

Intro
Moderately ♩ = 100

(Guitar)

Verse

I'll nev - er be...

1.

2.

Bridge

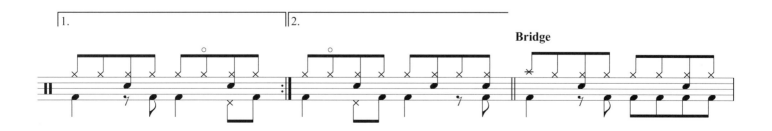

Verse

I'll nev - er be...

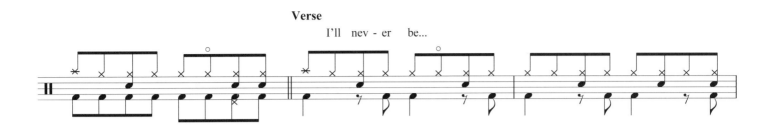

Bridge

Guitar Solo

Verse

You can   put me out...

Outro

I'll nev - er   be...

Beat It

Words and Music by Michael Jackson

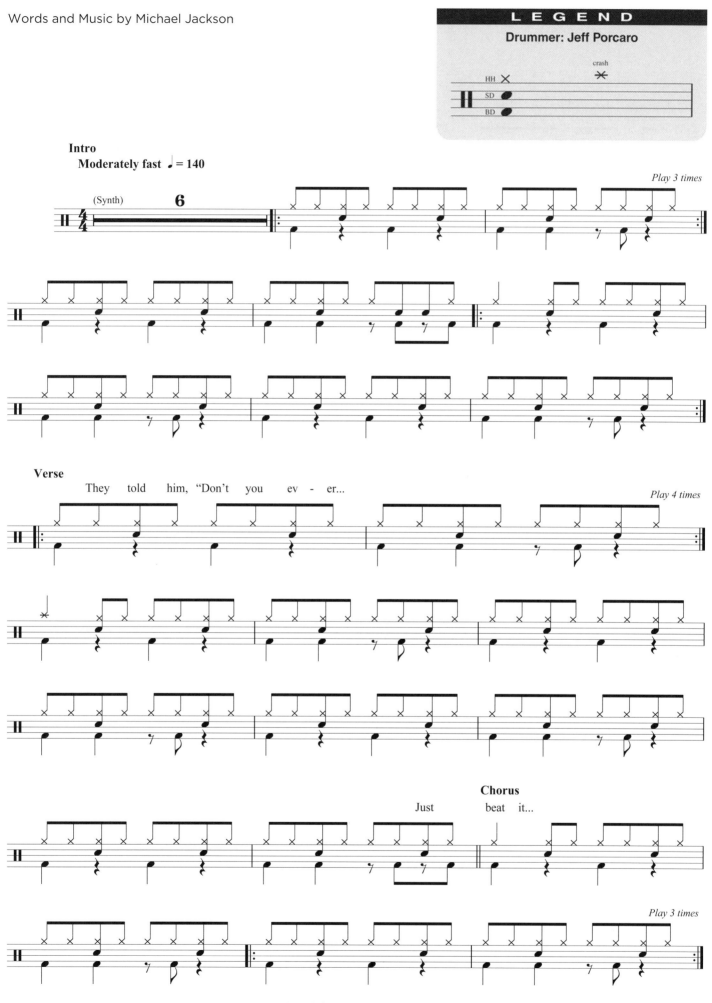

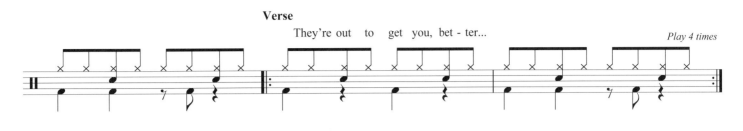

Verse

They're out to get you, bet - ter...

Play 4 times

Chorus

Just   beat it...

Play 4 times

Bridge

...beat it.

Play 3 times

Beat it.

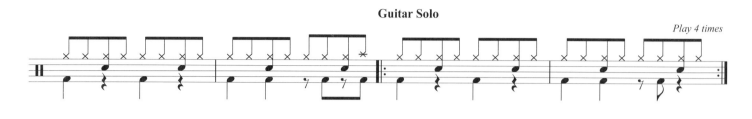

Guitar Solo

Chorus

Beat it...

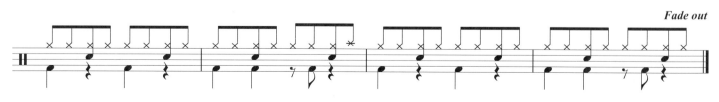

Come Together

Words and Music by John Lennon and Paul McCartney

Intro
Moderately slow Rock ♩ = 82

Verse

Here come ol' flat - top, he come...   ...got to be a jok - er, he just

Play 3 times

do what he please.

Interlude

Play 4 times

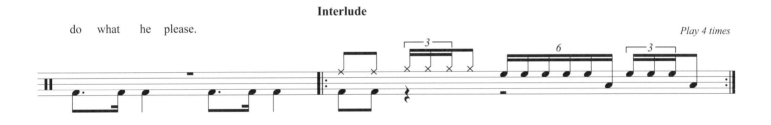

Verse

He wear no shoe-shine, he got...   One thing I can tell you is you

Play 3 times

got to be free.   **Chorus**
Come to - geth - er,   right now,   o - ver me.

Interlude

Verse

He bag pro - duc - tion, he got...　　　　　　Hold you　in his arm-chair, you can

Play 3 times

Chorus

feel his dis - ease.　Come to-geth - er,　　right　now,　　o - ver me.

Right!

Electric Piano Solo

Play 3 times

Guitar Solo

Verse

He rol - ler coast - er,　he got...　　　　　　Got to　be good look - in' 'cause he's

Play 3 times

Chorus

so hard to see.   Come to-geth - er,   right   now,   o - ver me.

Interlude

Play 3 times

Outro

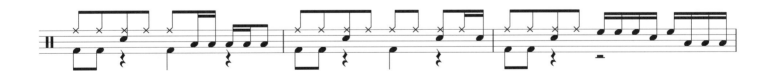

Fade out

Blitzkrieg Bop

Words and Music by Jeffrey Hyman, John Cummings,
Douglas Colvin and Thomas Erdelyi

Verse

% Bridge

Hey,   ho,   let's   go...

They're

Verse

form-in' in a straight   line...

2nd time, D.S. al Coda
(take repeat)

4th time, To Coda ⊕

⊕ Coda

Outro
Hey,   ho,

let's   go.   Hey,   ho,   let's   go.
Play 3 times

Brick House

Words and Music by Lionel Richie, Ronald LaPread, Walter Orange,
Milan Williams, Thomas McClary and William King

Verse

She knows she's got ev - 'ry - thing...

Chorus

1.

2.

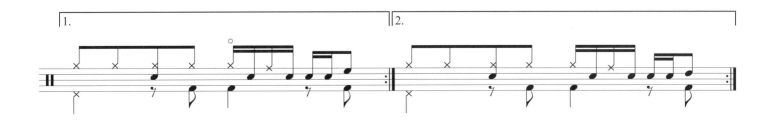

Verse

The clothes she wears,   her   sex - y ways...

Chorus

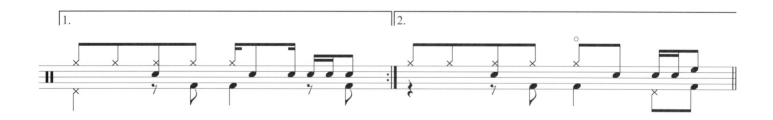

Bridge

Chorus

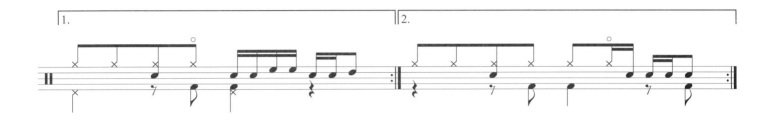

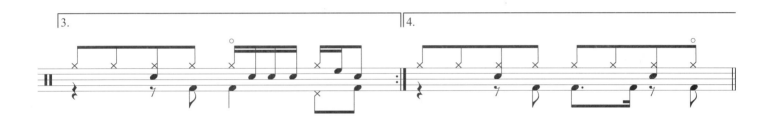

Outro

Repeat and fade

Cissy Strut

By Arthur Neville, Leo Nocentelli,
George Porter and Joseph Modeliste, Jr.

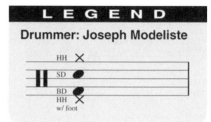
Moderately slow Funk ♩ = 88

Play 6 times

Play 5 times

Play 6 times

Play 6 times

Begin fade   **Fade out**

Clocks

Words and Music by Guy Berryman, Jon Buckland,
Will Champion and Chris Martin

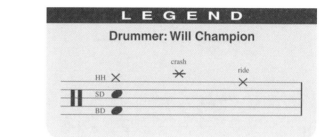
Intro
Moderately ♩ = 130

(Piano)   **8**

Verse

The   lights   go   out,   and   I   can't   be   saved...

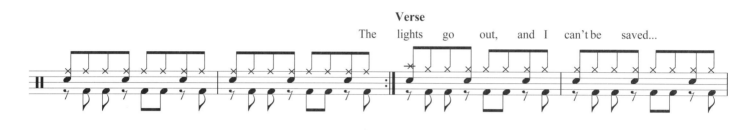

6th time, To Coda ⊕

Play 3 times

Chorus

D.S. al Coda
(take repeats)

⊕ **Coda**

Chorus

Play 4 times

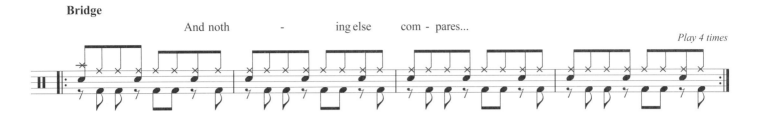

Bridge

And noth   -   ing else   com - pares...

Play 4 times

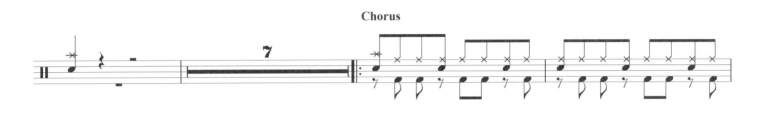

Chorus

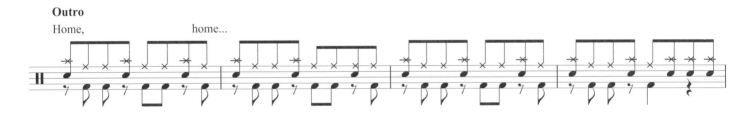

1., 2., 3.   4.

Outro

Home,   home...

Begin fade   *Fade out*

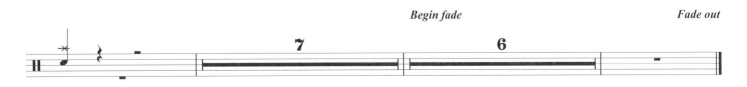

Cold Sweat, Pt. 1

Words and Music by James Brown and Alfred James Ellis

Intro
Moderate Funk ♩ = 112

Ha!

I don't

Verse

care,   ha,   a - bout your past.

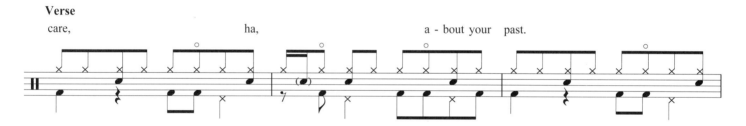

I just   want,   oh,   our love to

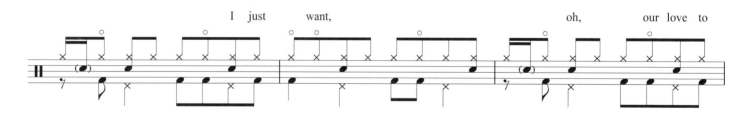

last.   Uh.   I don't care,   dar - lin',

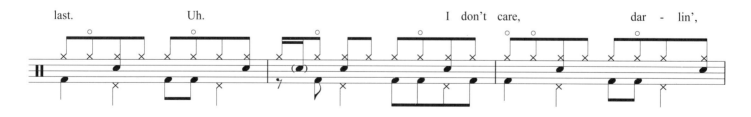

a - bout your   thoughts.   Ha,   uh.   I just

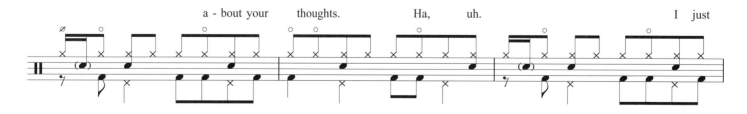

want   to sat - is - fy your thoughts.

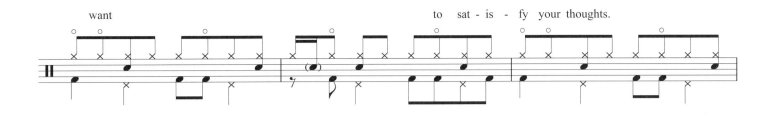

Chorus

Oh.   When ya kiss   me,

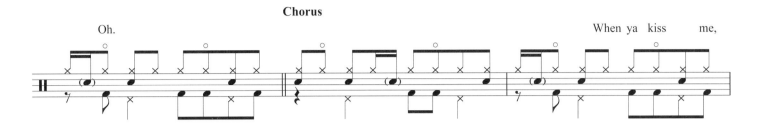

when ya miss   me.

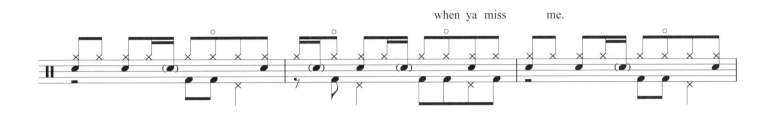

Hold   my   hand,   make me un -

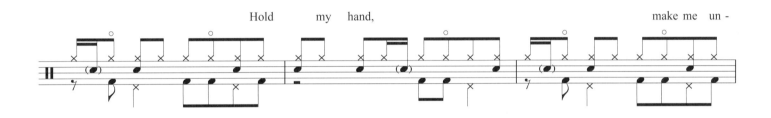

der -   stand.   I break out

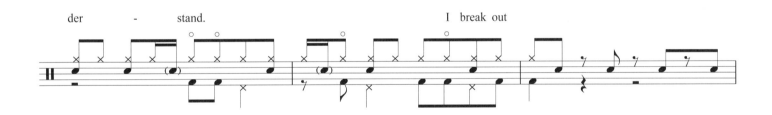

in a cold   sweat.   Oh.

Interlude

Uh.   Oh.

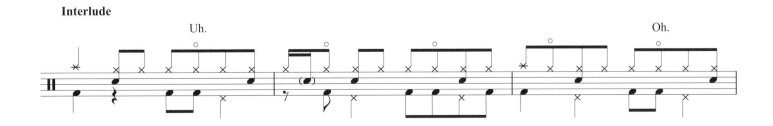

Verse

I don't care a - bout your

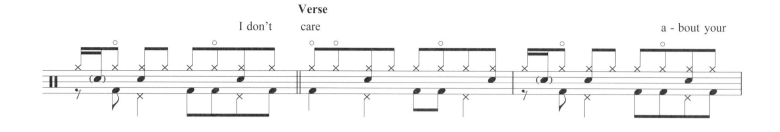

wants. I just wan- na, ha,

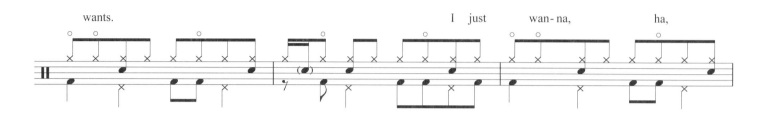

tell you 'bout your do's and don'ts. I don't

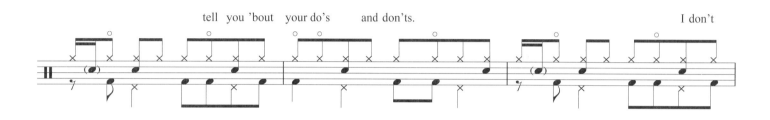

care a - bout the way you treat me, dar - lin'.

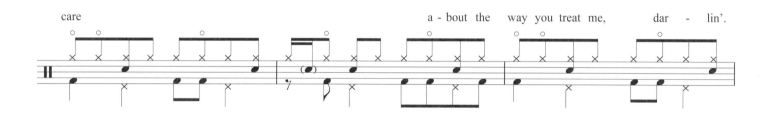

Ha! I just want, ha, to un -

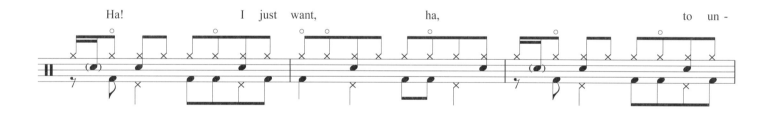

Chorus

der-stand me, hon - ey. Oh.

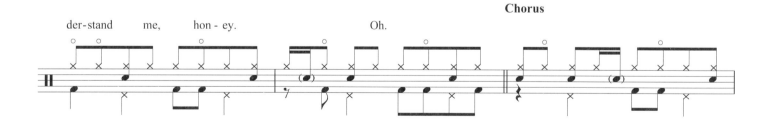

When ya kiss me, when ya miss

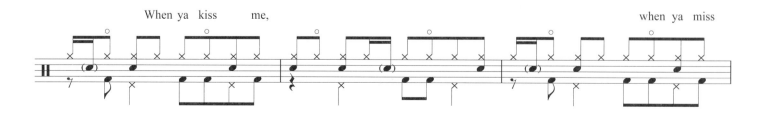

44

me.   You hold   me tight.

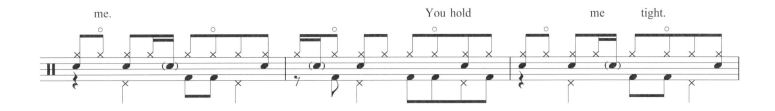

Make ev   -   'ry-thing al   -   right.   I break out

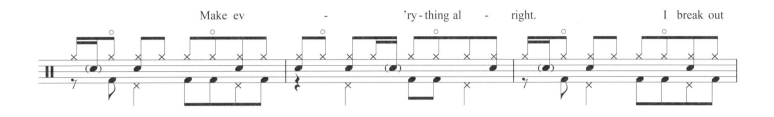

in a   cold   sweat.   Ha!

Outro

Ma   - ce- o,   come on   now,   broth-

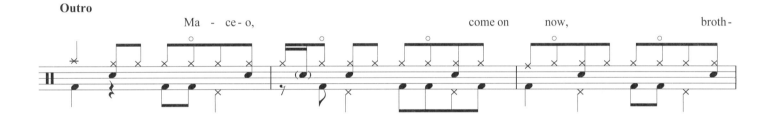

er,   put it,   put it where it's at now.

Begin fade

Ah.   Let 'em have it.

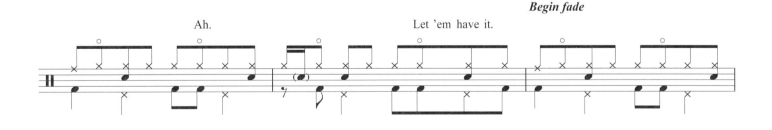

Fade out

Uh!

Dance, Dance

Words and Music by Patrick Stumph, Peter Wentz,
Andrew Hurley and Joseph Trohman

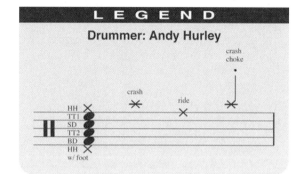

Intro
Moderately ♩ = 115
Double-time feel

Play 3 times

Verse

1. She says she's no good...

Play 3 times

Pre-Chorus

𝄋 Chorus

2nd time, double-time feel

Dance,   dance,   we're fall-ing a - part...

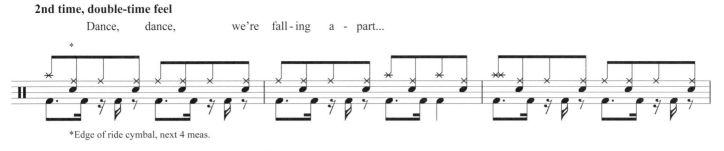

*Edge of ride cymbal, next 4 meas.

To Coda ⊕

Verse

2. You   al - ways fold   just...

Pre-Chorus

End double-time feel

D.S. al Coda

⊕ **Coda**

End double-time feel

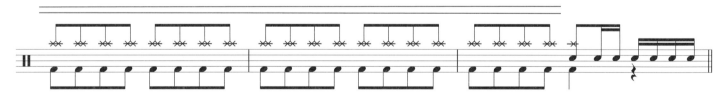

Bridge

Why   don't   you   show   me...

Play 3 times

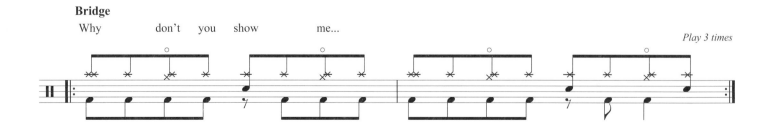

Double-time feel

Chorus

Dance,   dance,   we're   fall-ing   a - part...

*Edge of ride cymbal, next 4 meas.

Outro

1., 2.   3.

Free Fallin'

Words and Music by Tom Petty and Jeff Lynne

Intro
Moderately ♩ = 85

Verse

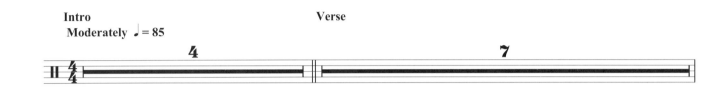

And it's a

Verse

long   day...   *Play 3 times*

Chorus

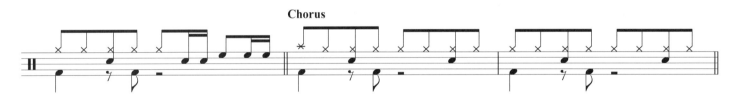

Verse

Play 3 times

Play 3 times

Chorus

Interlude

Verse

Chorus

Outro-Chorus

Give It Away

Words and Music by Anthony Kiedis, Flea,
John Frusciante and Chad Smith

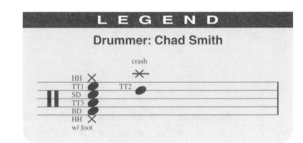

Intro
Moderate Funk ♩ = 92

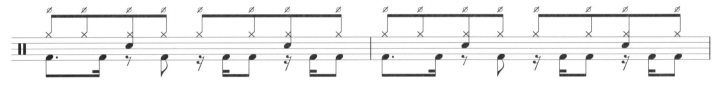

𝄋 **Verse**

What I've got, you've got to give it to your ma - ma...

2nd time, substitute Fill 1
3rd time, substitute Fill 2

Play 6 times

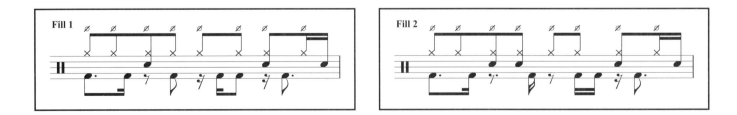

2nd & 3rd times, substitute Fill 1

Chorus

Give it a-way, give it a-way, give it a-way now...

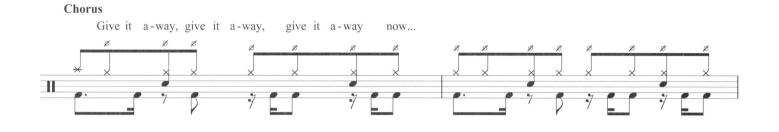

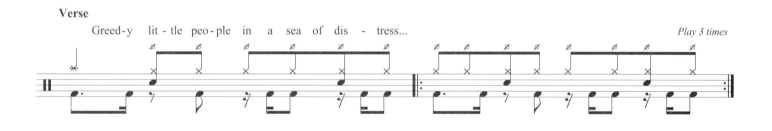

Verse

Greed-y lit-tle peo-ple in a sea of dis - tress...   *Play 3 times*

Play 3 times

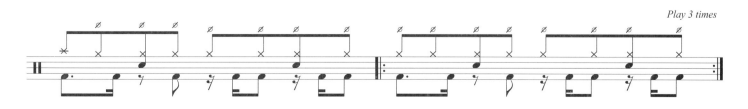

Chorus

Give it a-way, give it a-way,   give it a-way   now...

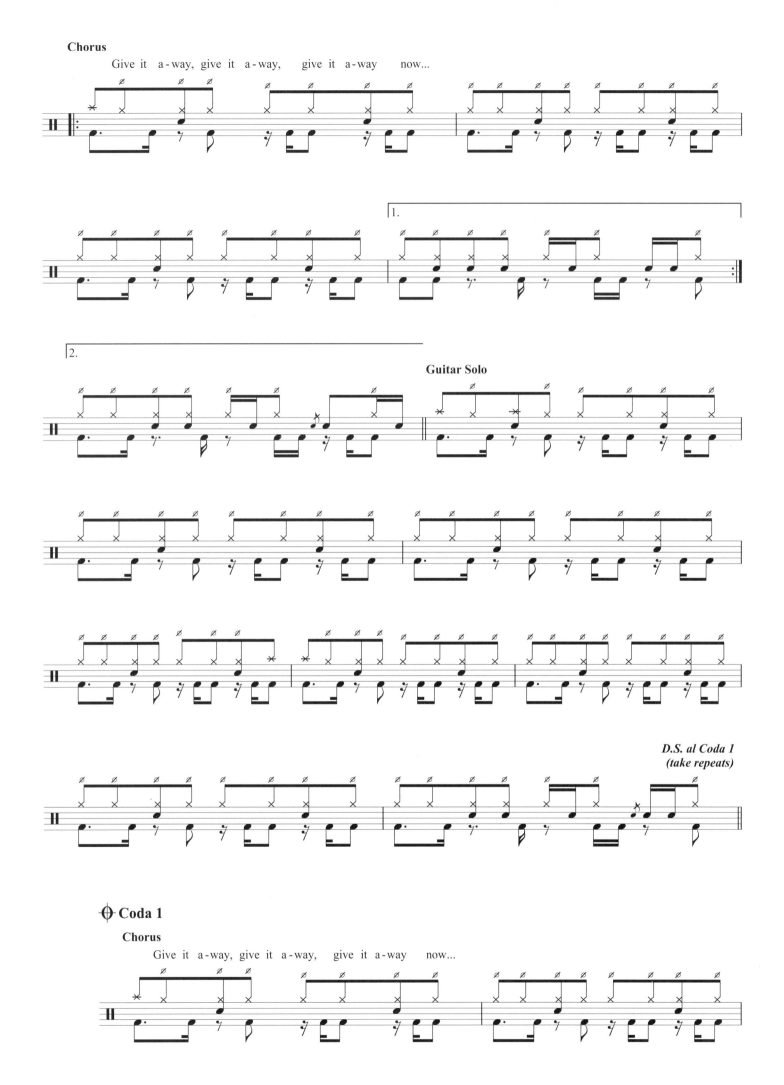

Guitar Solo

D.S. al Coda 1
(take repeats)

Coda 1

Chorus

Give it a-way, give it a-way,   give it a-way   now...

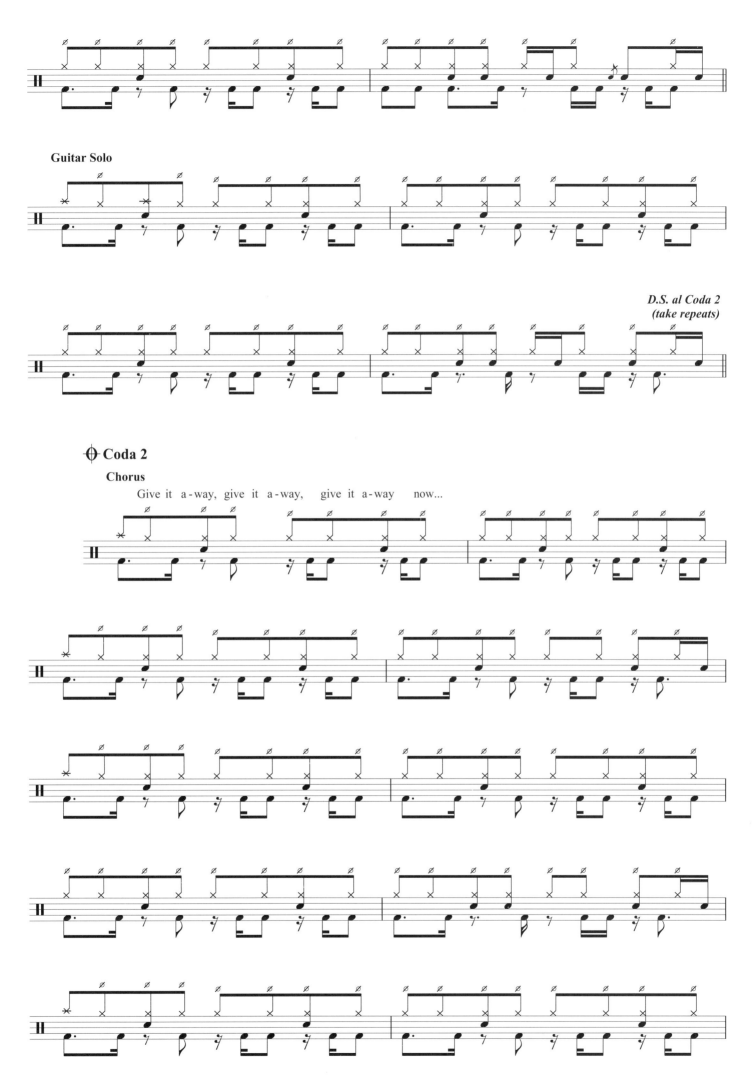

Guitar Solo

D.S. al Coda 2
(take repeats)

Coda 2

Chorus

Give it a-way, give it a-way, give it a-way now...

Hurts So Good

Words and Music by John Mellencamp and George Green

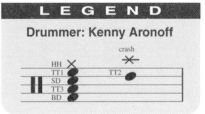

Chorus

...hurt so good.

To Coda ⊕

D.S. al Coda
(take repeats)

⊕ **Coda**

Bridge

I ain't talk - in' no big   deals...

58

Chorus

Hurts so good...

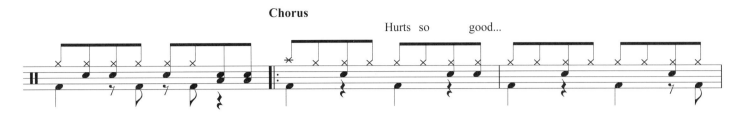

1.

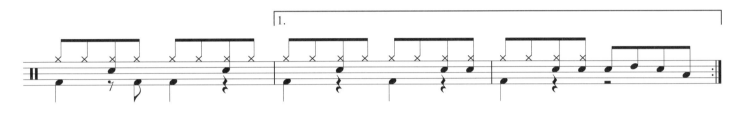

2.

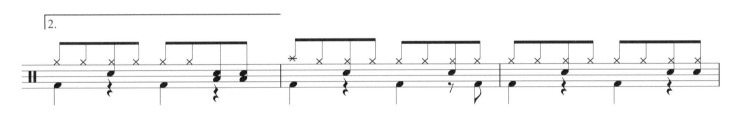

Outro

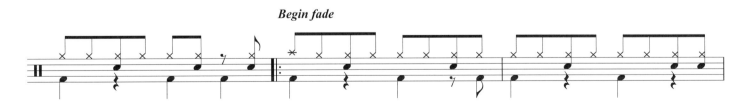

Begin fade

1.

2.

Fade out

Good Times Bad Times

Words and Music by Jimmy Page, John Paul Jones and John Bonham

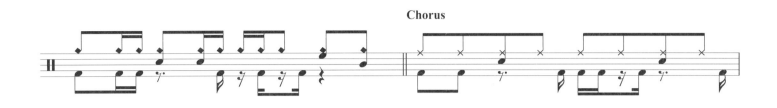

Chorus

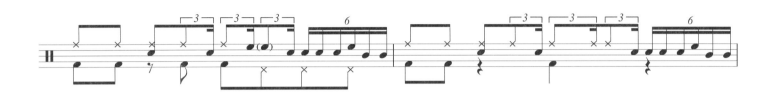

Verse

Six - teen, I fell in love...

Chorus

Guitar Solo

Chorus

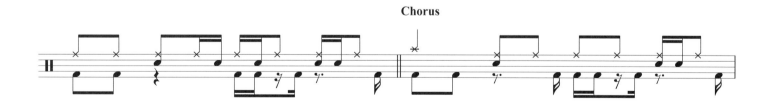

Outro

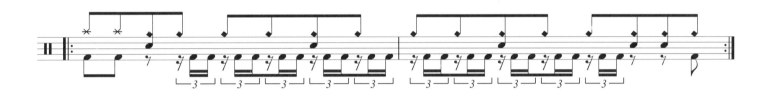

Begin fade   *Fade out*

Hot Fun in the Summertime

Words and Music by Sylvester Stewart

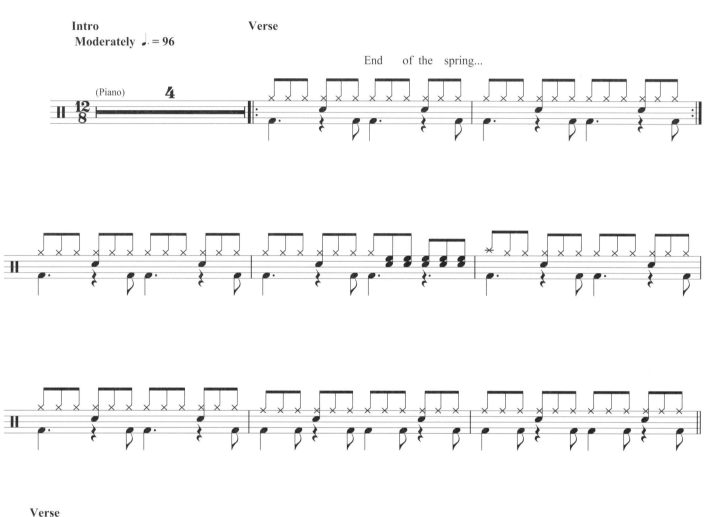

Intro
Moderately ♩. = 96   **Verse**

(Piano)

End   of the   spring...

Verse

That's when I   have...

Pre-Chorus

I cloud nine   when I want...

Play 4 times

Chorus

Hot   fun   in   the sum - mer - time.

Play 4 times

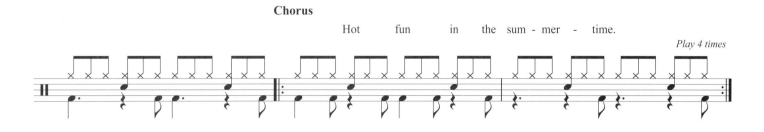

Verse

First   of the   fall...

Pre-Chorus

Repeat and fade

Outro-Chorus

Hot   fun   in   the sum - mer - time...

Play 4 times

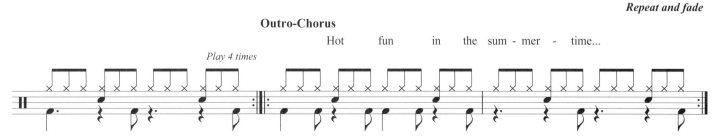

65

Interstate Love Song

Words and Music by Scott Weiland, Dean DeLeo, Robert DeLeo and Eric Kretz

Intro
Moderately slow ♩ = 84

Play 3 times

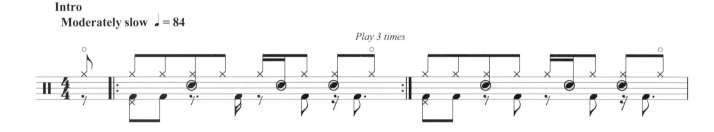

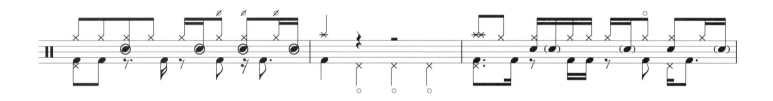

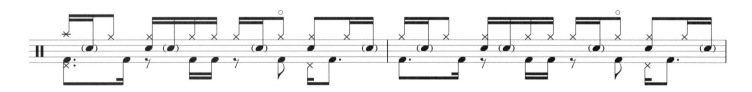

Verse
1. Wait - in'   on a

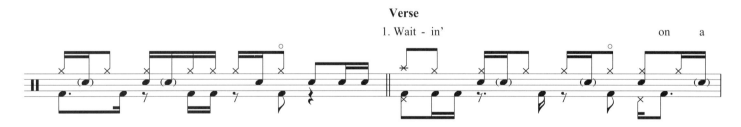

Sun - day af - ter - noon...

Interlude

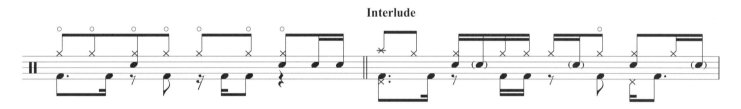

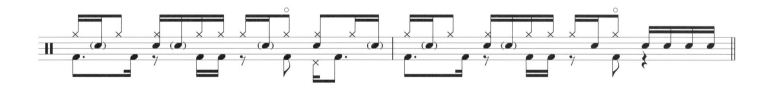

Chorus

Leav - in'   on a   south - ern train...

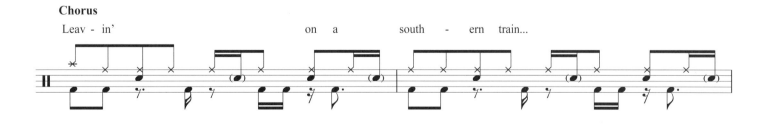

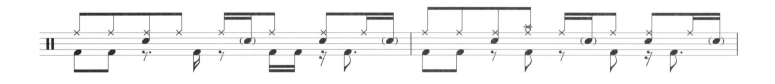

Interlude

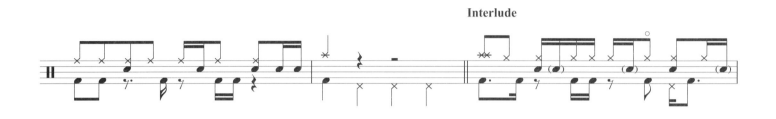

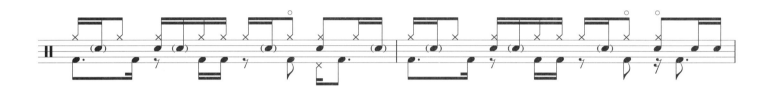

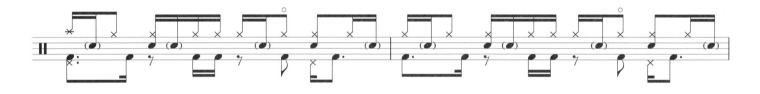

Verse

2. Breath - in'   is the

hard - est thing   to   do...

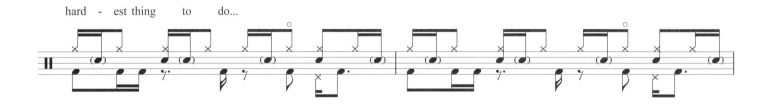

Chorus

Leav - in'   on a

south - ern train...

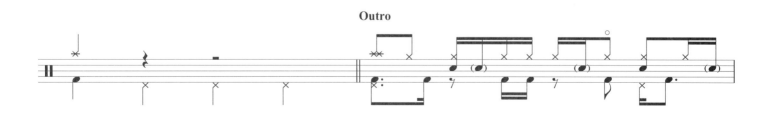

Outro

La Grange

Words and Music by Billy F Gibbons, Dusty Hill and Frank Lee Beard

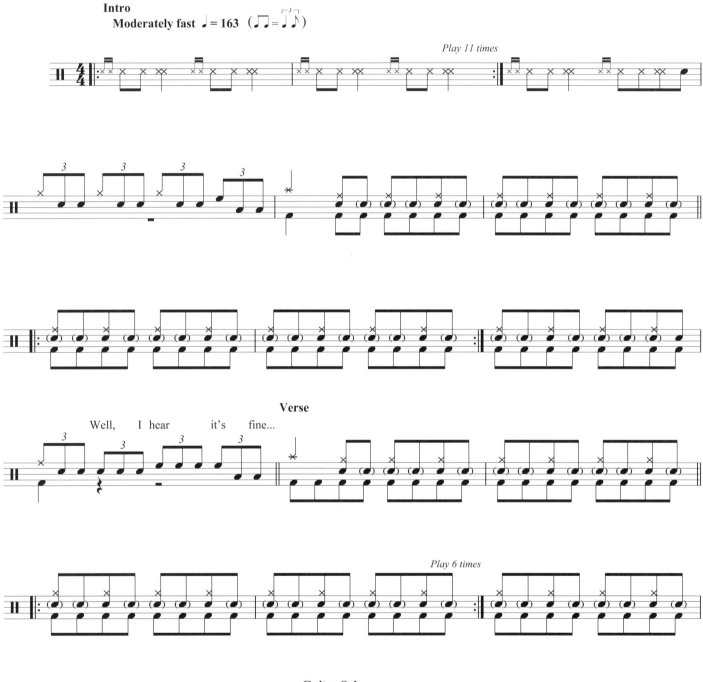

Play 14 times

Interlude

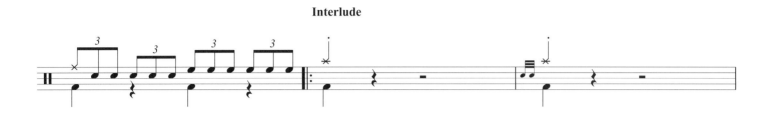

Guitar Solo

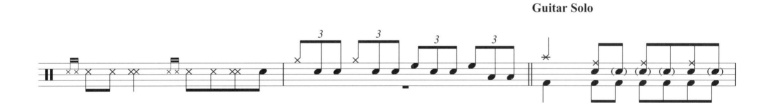

Play 6 times

Begin fade

Play 7 times

Repeat and fade

Learn to Fly

Words and Music by Taylor Hawkins, Nate Mendel and Dave Grohl

Make my way back home when I learn to fly

Interlude
high...

Verse
I think I'm dy - in' mis - sing...

Play 6 times

74

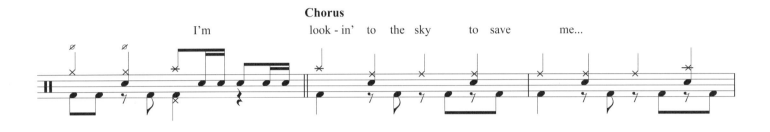

Chorus

I'm   look - in' to the sky   to save   me...

Bridge

Fly   a - long with me...

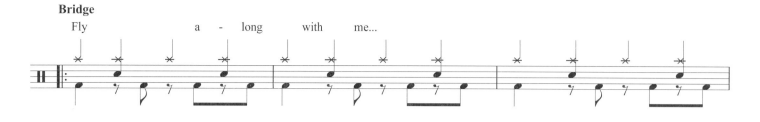

1.

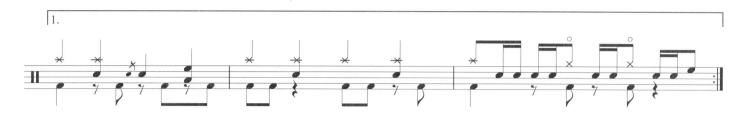

2.

                                                I'm

Chorus

look - in' to the sky   to save   me...

Chorus

Look- in' to the sky   to save

me...

Outro

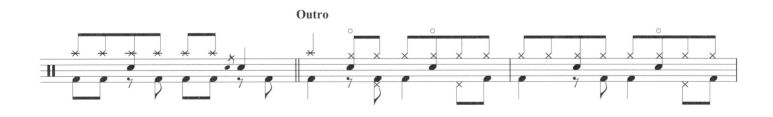

Late in the Evening

Words and Music by Paul Simon

To Coda ⊕

1.

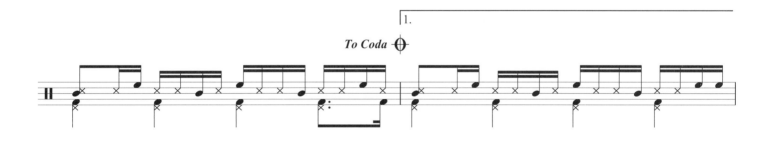

2.

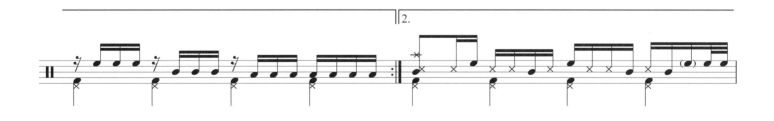

3.

Interlude

D.S. al Coda

Coda

Interlude

Play 3 times

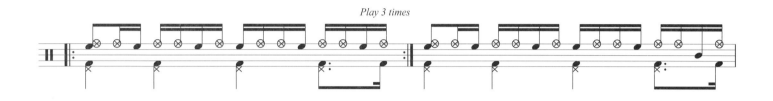

Play 3 times

Play 3 times

Outro

Repeat and fade

Locked Out of Heaven

Words and Music by Bruno Mars, Ari Levine and Philip Lawrence

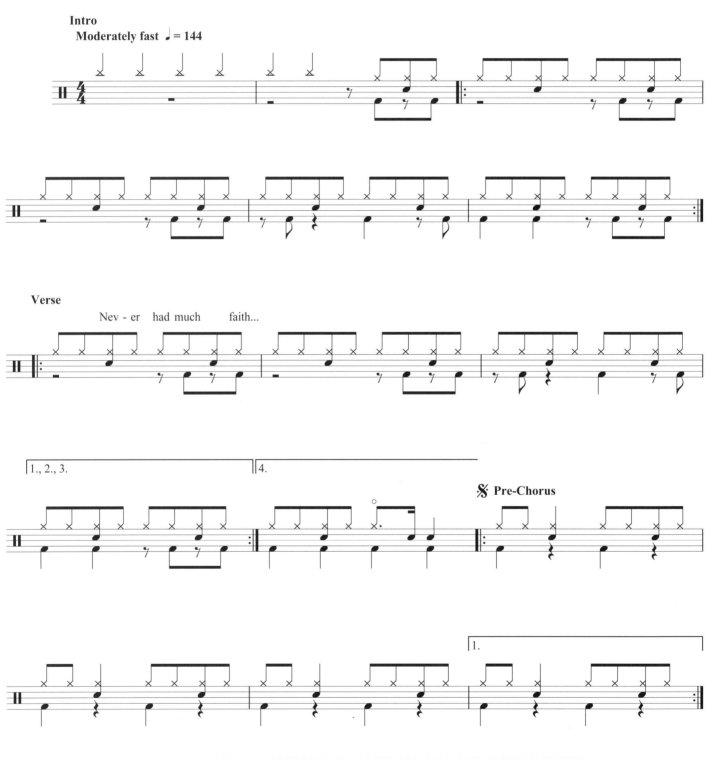

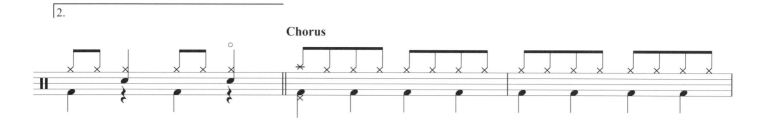

Chorus

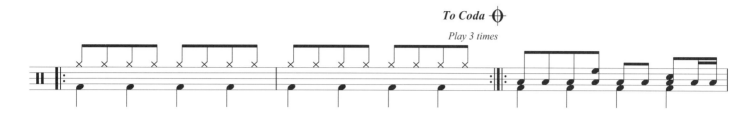

To Coda ⊕

Play 3 times

|1., 2., 3. |4.

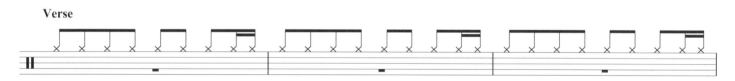

Verse

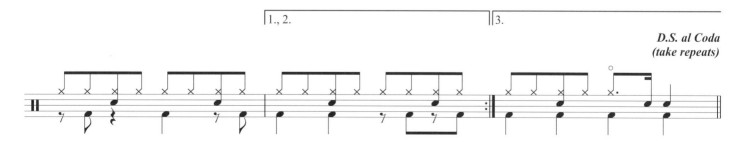

|1., 2. |3.

D.S. al Coda
(take repeats)

⊕ **Coda**

Play 3 times

Bridge

Chorus

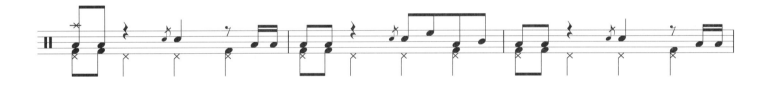

Outro

Mr. Brownstone

Words and Music by W. Axl Rose, Slash,
Izzy Stradlin', Duff McKagan and Steven Adler

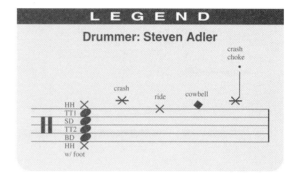

Intro
Moderately ♩ = 105

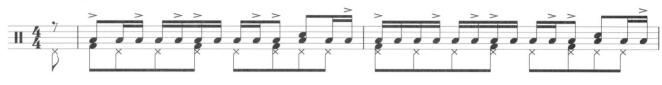

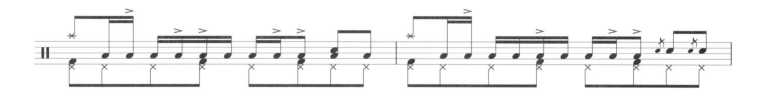

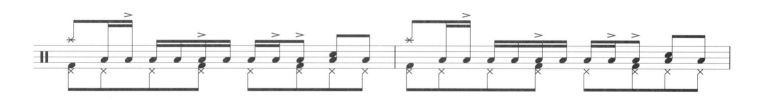

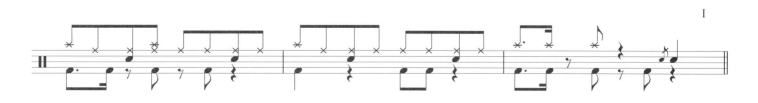

Verse

get up   a-round   sev-en...

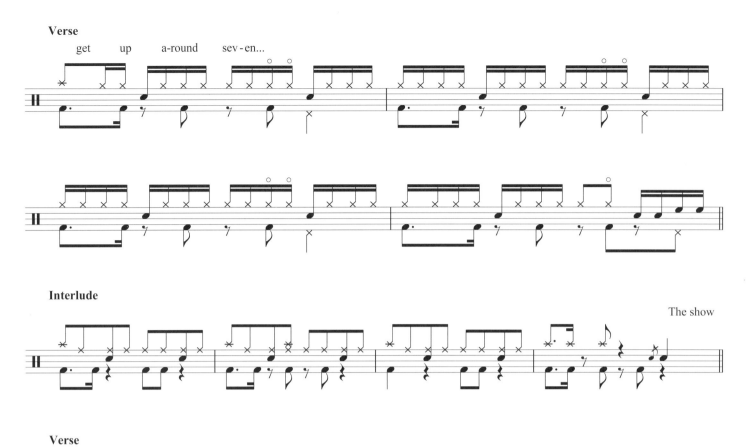

Interlude

The show

Verse

u - s'al - ly starts   a-round   sev - en...

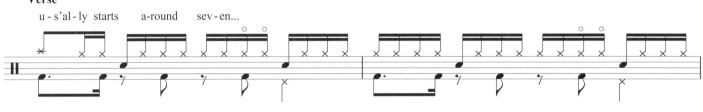

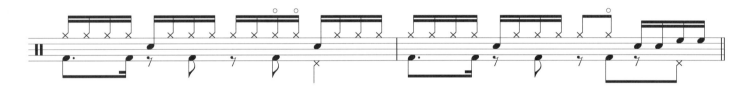

Chorus

We've   been   danc - in'   with...

I

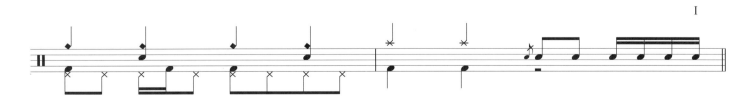

Bridge

used ta do a lit - tle, but a lit - tle would - n't do...

Chorus

We've been danc - in' with...

Guitar Solo

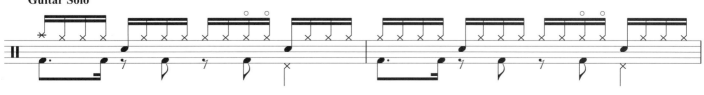

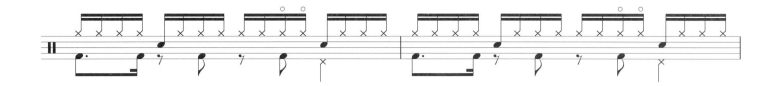

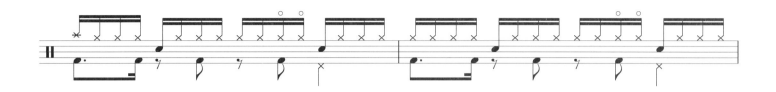

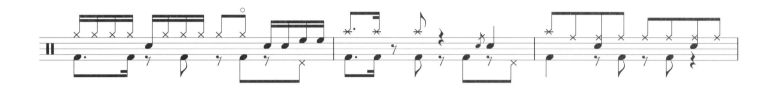

Interlude

Verse

Now I get up   a-round when-ev - er...

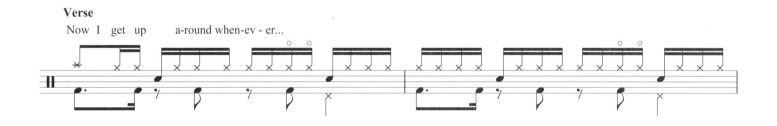

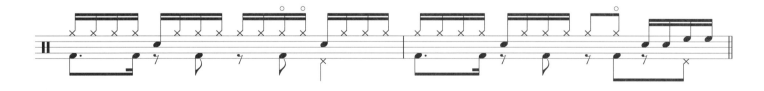

Bridge

used ta do a lit - tle, but a lit - tle would-n't do...

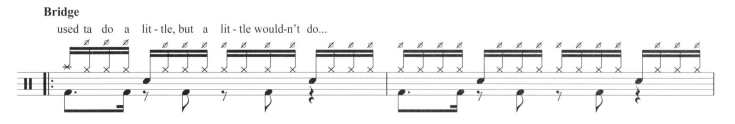

Chorus

We've been danc - in' with...

Interlude

Outro

Free time

Lonely Boy

Words and Music by Dan Auerbach, Patrick Carney and Brian Burton

Lust for Life

Written by Iggy Pop and David Bowie

Intro
Moderately ♩ = 100
Double-time feel

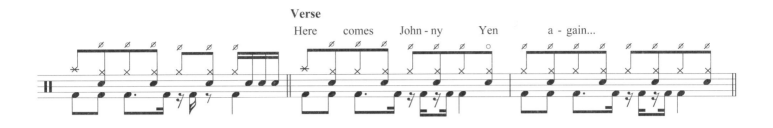

Verse

Here comes John - ny Yen a - gain...

Play 3 times

Verse

I'm worth   a   mil - lion in priz -

- es...

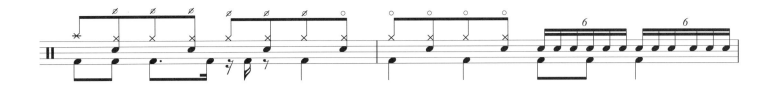

Chorus

Play 3 times   Well,
                                                                                    6

Verse
here   comes   John - ny   Yen   a - gain...

Play 3 times

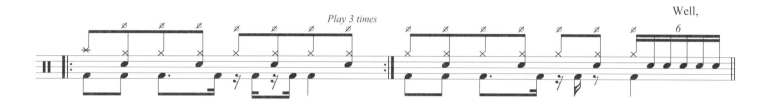

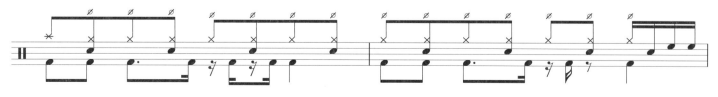

*Played as even sixteenth notes.

Outro

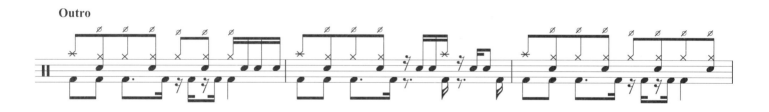

Begin fade

Fade out

Memphis Soul Stew

Words and Music by Curtis Ousley

Intro
Moderately ♩ = 113

Play 3 times

Play 3 times

Chorus

Play 4 times

Play 4 times

1., 2., 3.

4.

Repeat and fade

My Generation

Words and Music by Peter Townshend

Verse

Why don't you all f - fade a - way...

Interlude

Verse

Why don't you all f - fade

a - way...

Verse

Peo - ple   try   to

put   us   d - down...

Outro

Play 3 times

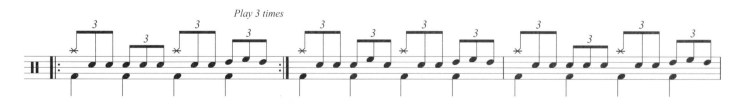

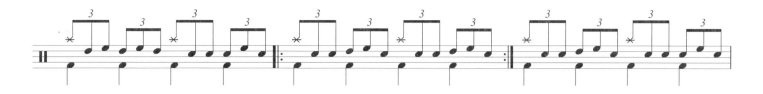

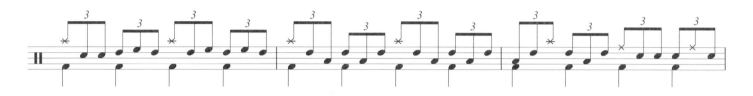

Play 3 times

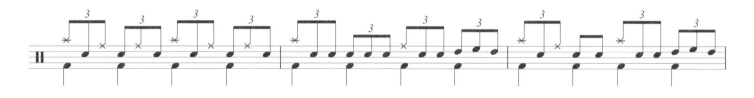

Play 3 times

Free time

My Name Is Jonas

Words and Music by Rivers Cuomo,
Patrick Wilson and Jason Cropper

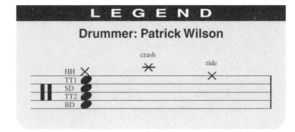

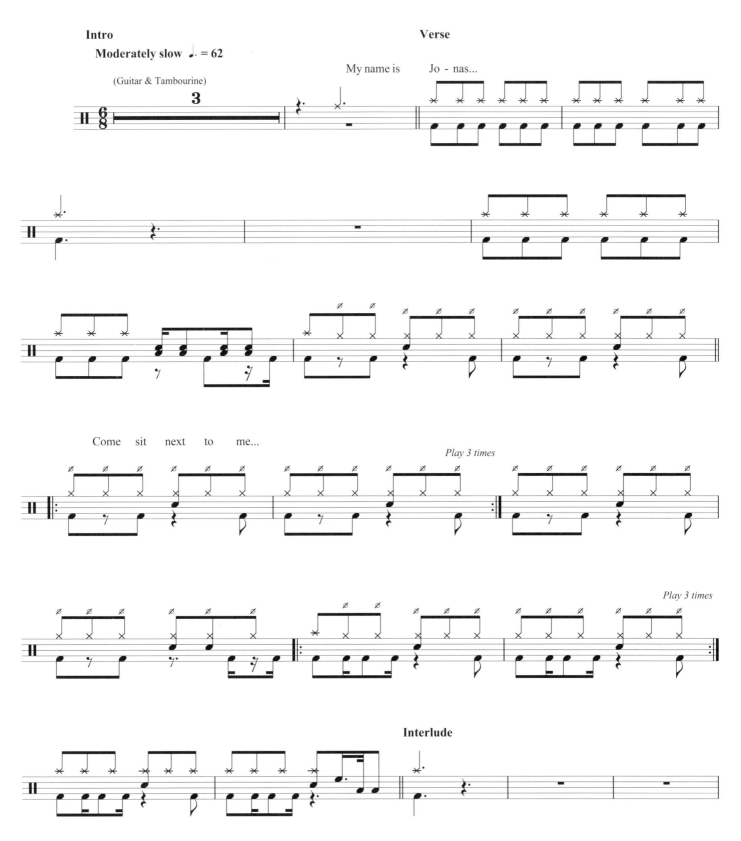

Verse

My name is We - peel...

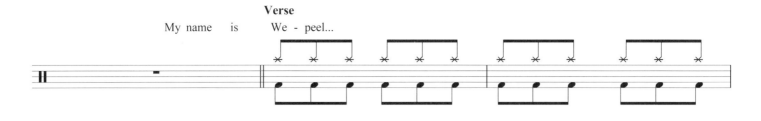

Play 3 times

Play 3 times

Chorus

The work - ers are go - ing home...

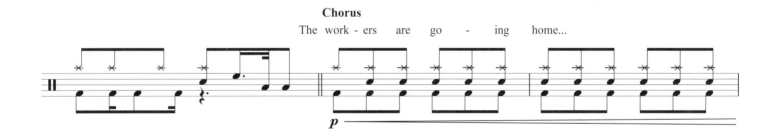

p

f

Interlude

Play 3 times

Chorus

Work - ers are go - ing home...

Play 5 times

Harmonica Solo

Play 3 times

Outro

Peg

Words and Music by Walter Becker and Donald Fagen

LEGEND — Drummer: Rick Marotta

Intro
Moderate Jazz-Rock ♩ = 117

I've seen your

Verse
pic - ture...

Play 5 times

I like your

Verse
pin - shot...

Play 10 times

Chorus
Peg,   it will come back to you...

Play 4 times

Interlude

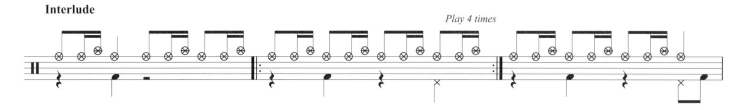

Play 4 times

Guitar Solo

Play 11 times

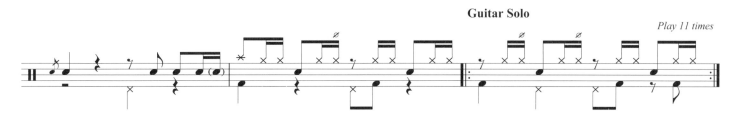

Verse

I like your pin - shot...

Play 11 times

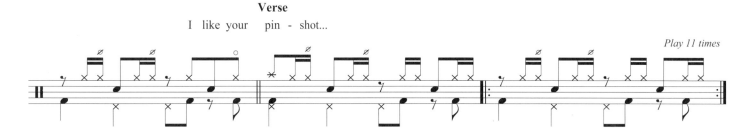

Outro-Chorus

Peg, it will come back to you...

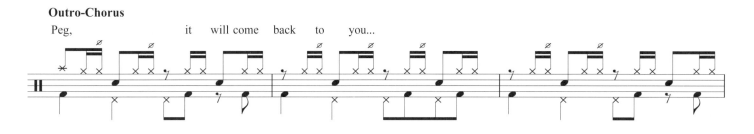

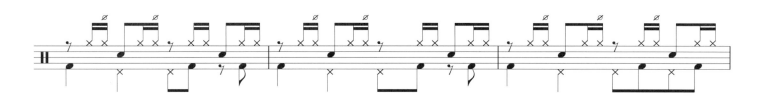

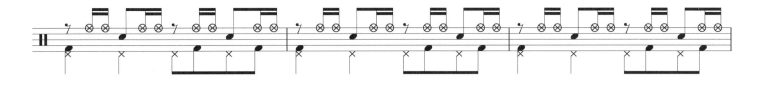

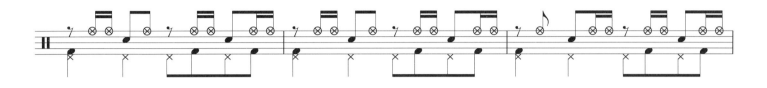

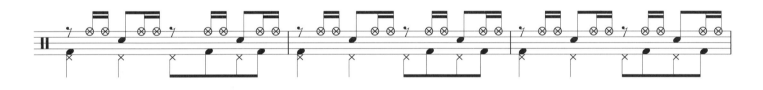

Begin fade

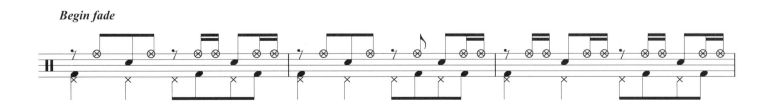

Fade out

No One Knows

Words and Music by Mark Lanegan, Josh Homme and Nick Oliveri

Intro
Fast ♩ = 172

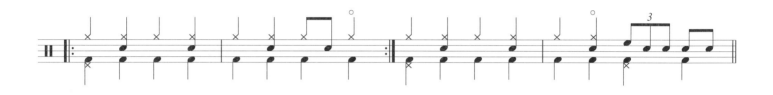

Verse

We get some rules to fol - low...

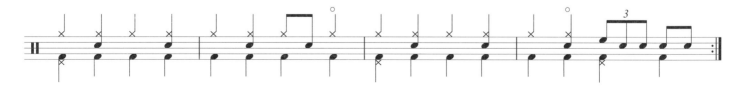

And I

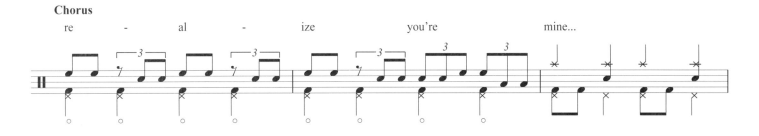

Chorus

re - al - ize you're mine...

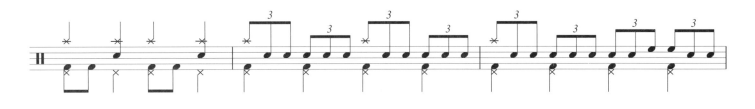

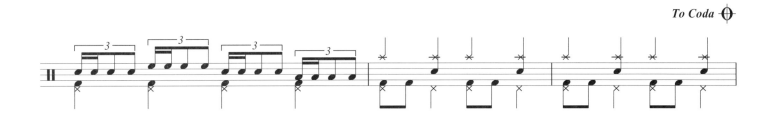

To Coda ⊕

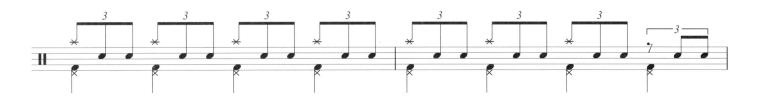

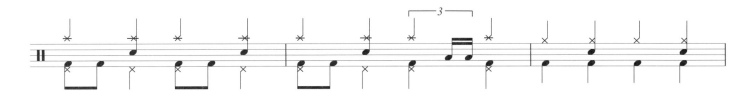

Coda

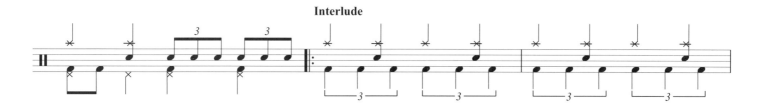

Interlude

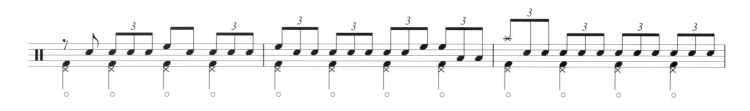

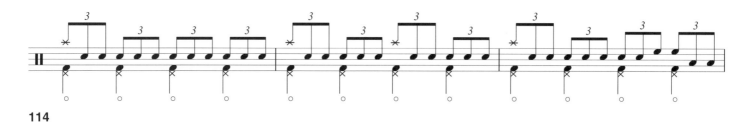

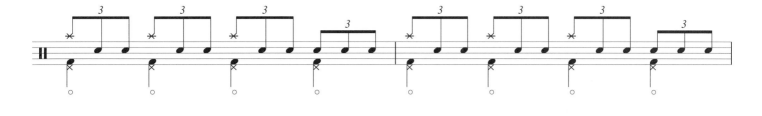

Outro

What   a   gift   here be - low...

Ride

Words and Music by Tyler Joseph

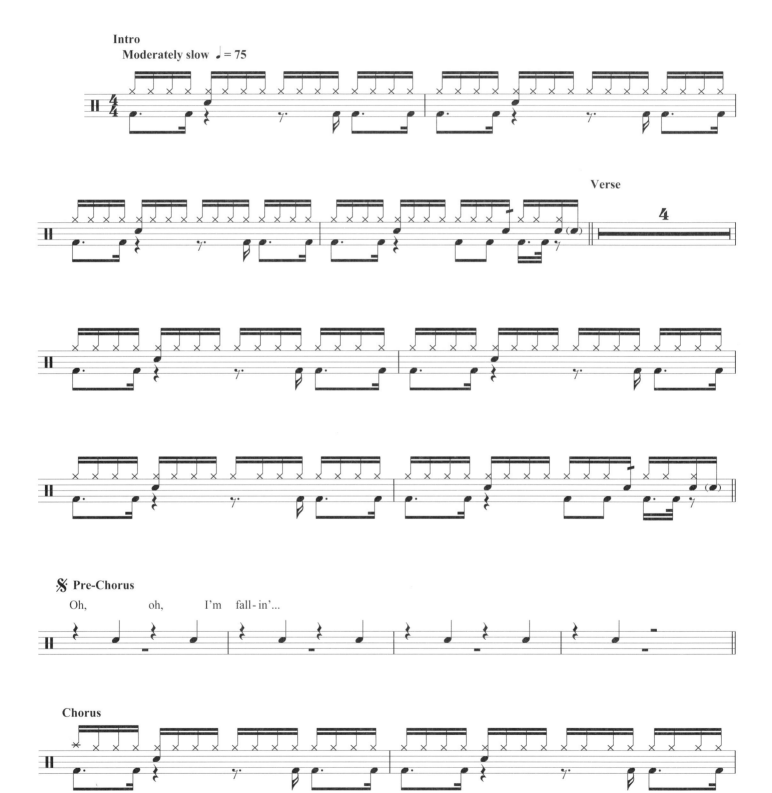

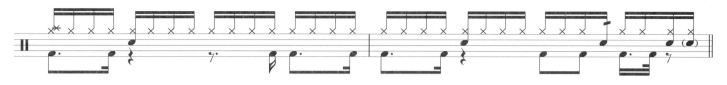

Verse

Play 3 times

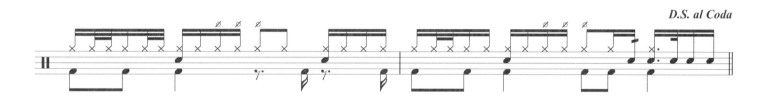

D.S. al Coda

⊕ **Coda**

Bridge

I've been think-in' too much...

Pre-Chorus

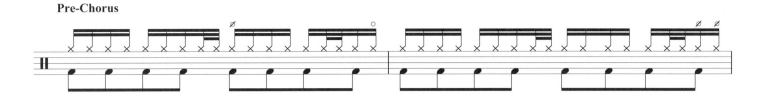

Chorus

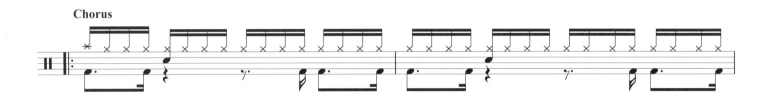

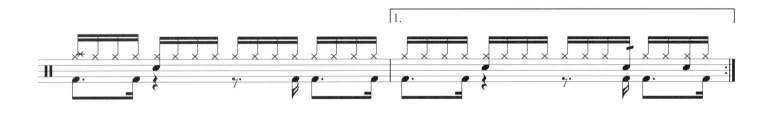

Rolling in the Deep

Words and Music by Adele Adkins and Paul Epworth

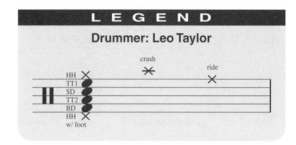

Verse

Ba - by,   I   have   no   sto - ry   to   be   told...

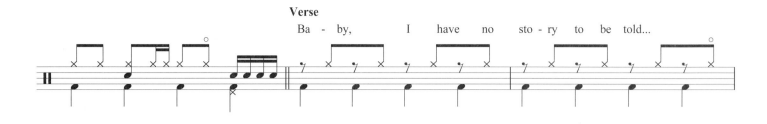

Pre-Chorus

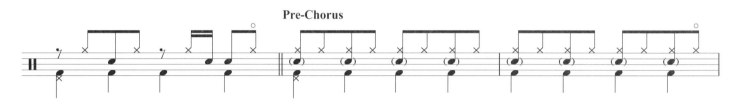

D.S. al Coda

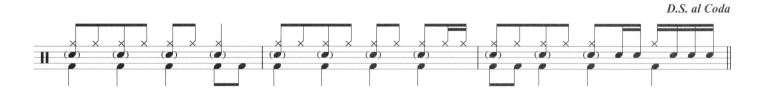

Coda

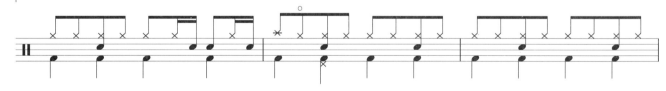

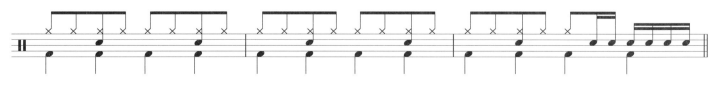

Verse
Throw your soul through ev-er-y o - pen door...

Run to the Hills

Words and Music by Steve Harris

Intro
Moderate Rock ♩ = 120

Verse

White man came...

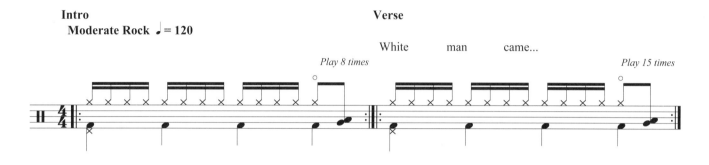

Faster ♩ = 172

...be set free.

𝄋 Verse

Rid - ing through dust clouds...

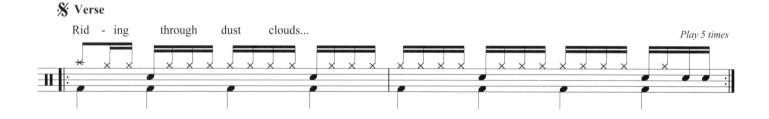

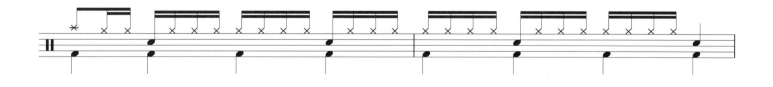

Chorus

Run   to   the

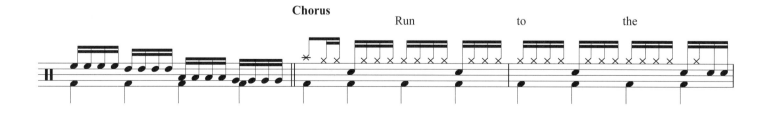

hills...

To Coda ⊕

D.S. al Coda
(take repeats)

⊕ **Coda**

Guitar Solo

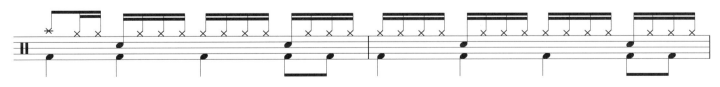

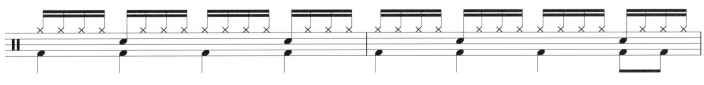

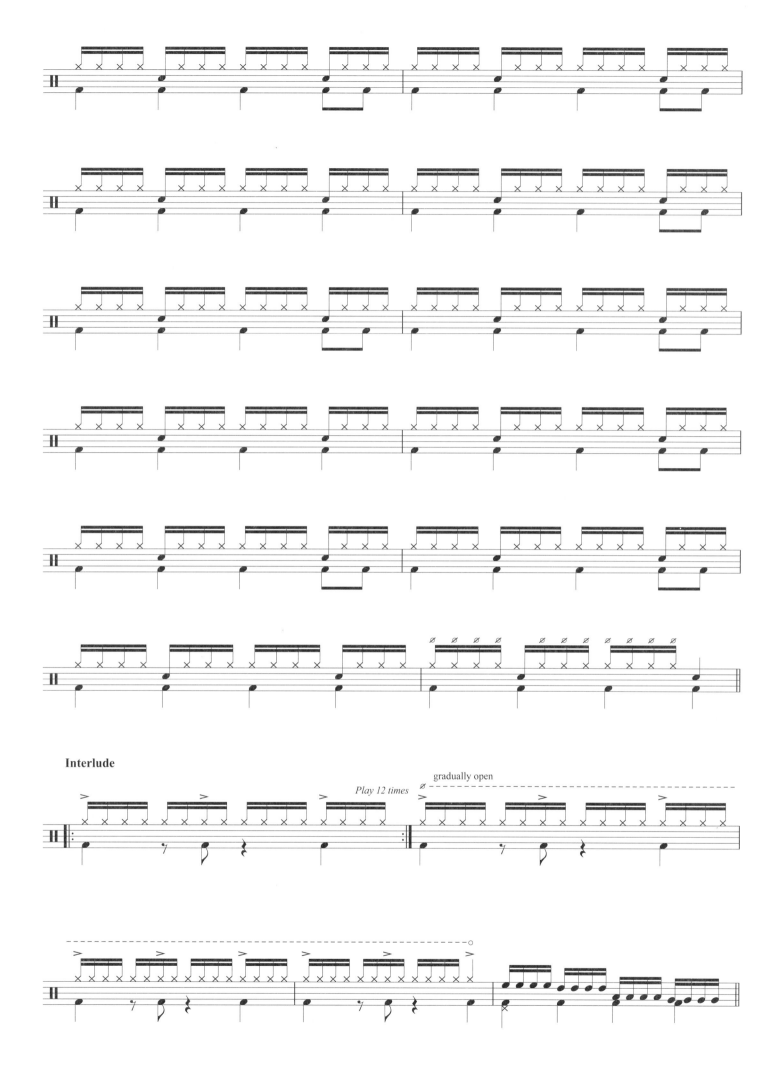

Interlude

Chorus

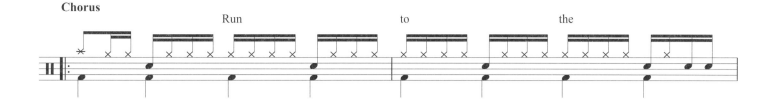

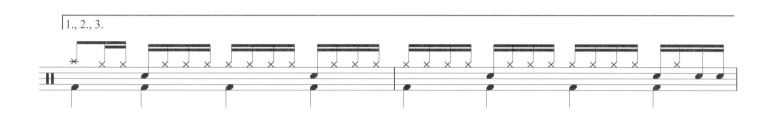

Sad but True

Words and Music by James Hetfield and Lars Ulrich

Intro
Moderately ♩ = 93

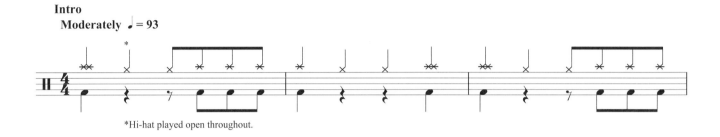

*Hi-hat played open throughout.

Slightly slower ♩ = 89

Play 3 times

Verse

Hey,   I'm your life...

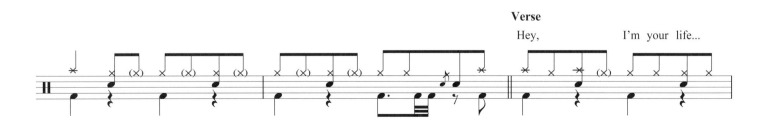

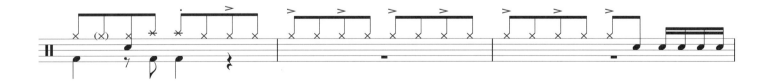

Chorus

I'm your dream,   make you real...

Verse

You,   you're my mask...

Chorus

I'm your dream,   make you real...

Interlude

Play 3 times

Guitar Solo

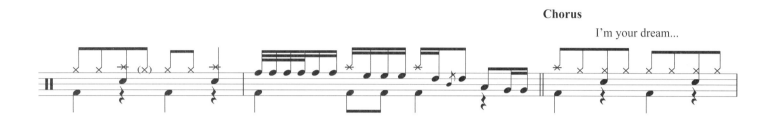

Chorus

I'm your dream...

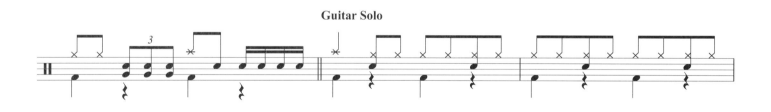

Guitar Solo

Verse

Hate, I'm your hate...

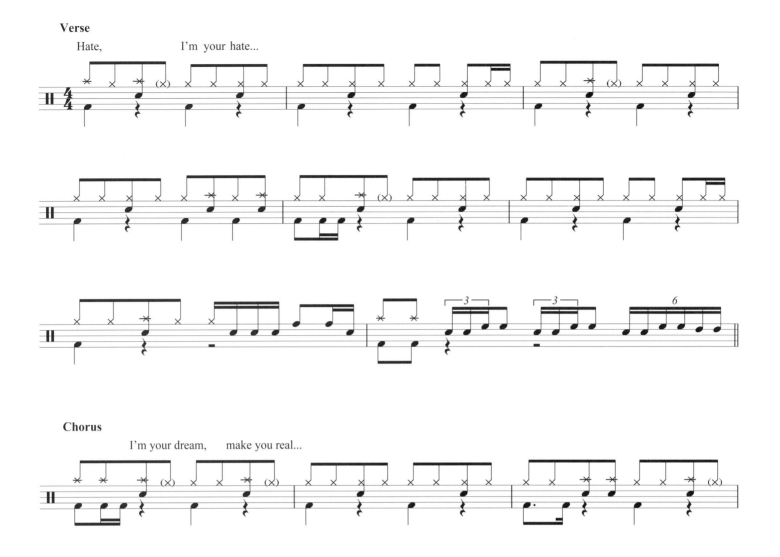

Chorus

I'm your dream, make you real...

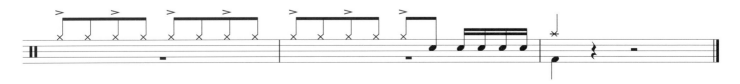

Should I Stay or Should I Go

Words and Music by Mick Jones and Joe Strummer

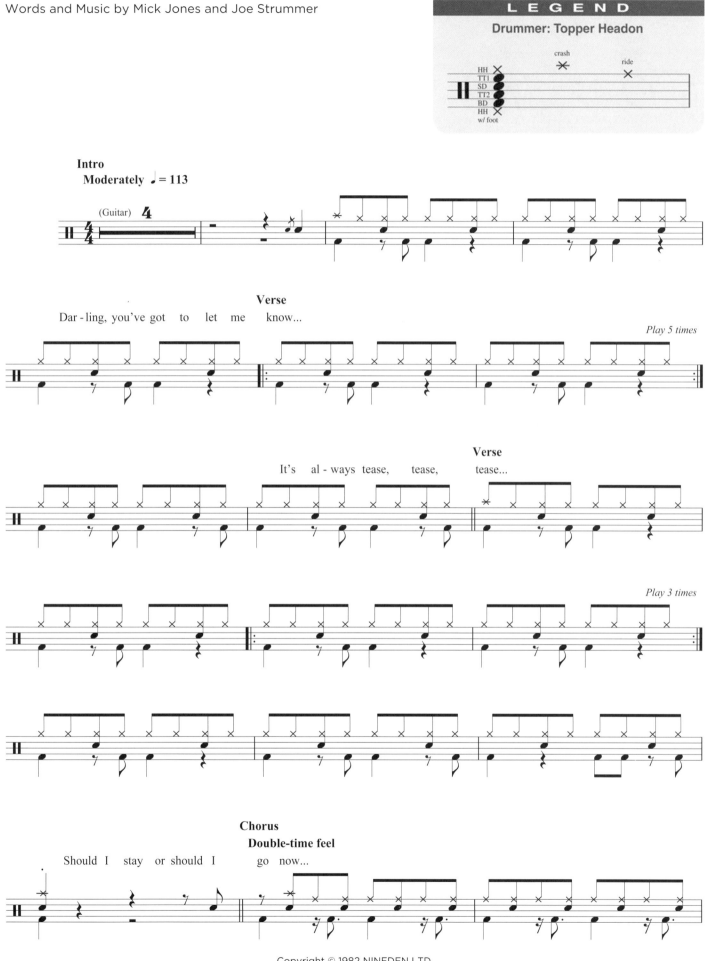

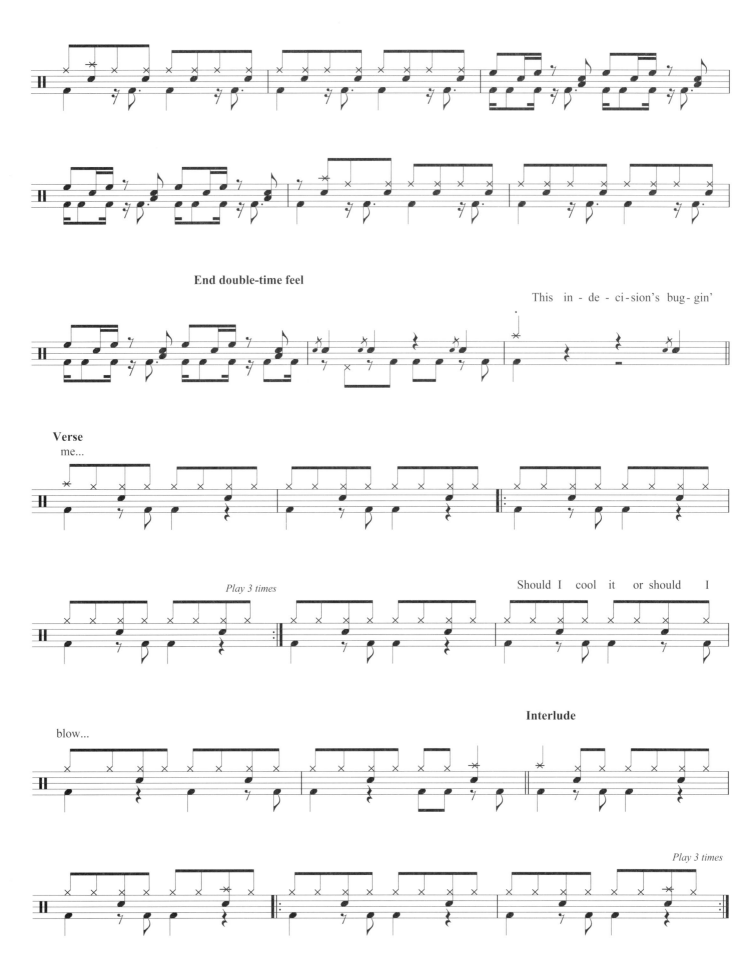

End double-time feel

This in - de - ci - sion's bug - gin'

Verse

me...

Play 3 times

Should I cool it or should I

Interlude

blow...

Play 3 times

Chorus
Double-time feel

Should I   stay   or   should I   go   now...

Outro-Chorus

Should   I   stay   or   should   I   go   now...

End double-time feel

The Seed

Words and Music by Tarik Collins and Cody Chestnutt

Chorus
I push my seed in her bush for life...

Ca-dil-

Verse
lac needs space to roam...

Play 3 times

Play 3 times

Verse

Play 3 times

Chorus

I push my seed in her bush for life...

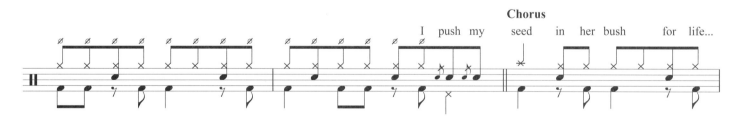

Bridge

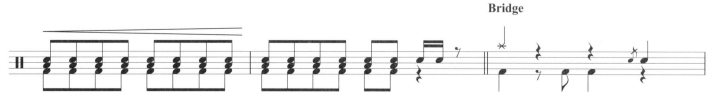

Chorus

I push my seed in her bush for life...

Outro

Shake It Off

Words and Music by Taylor Swift, Max Martin and Shellback

Pre-Chorus

Play 3 times

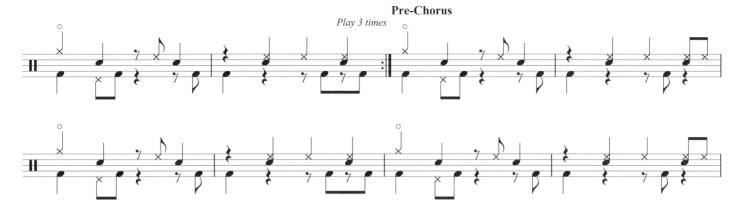

Chorus

Bridge

Play 3 times

1. | 2.

Chorus

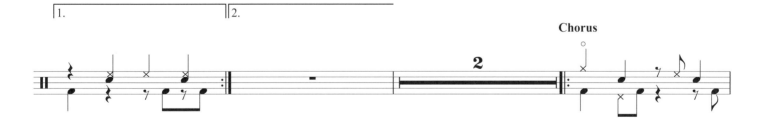

Play 4 times

Sing, Sing, Sing

Words and Music by Louis Prima

LEGEND

Drummer: Gene Krupa

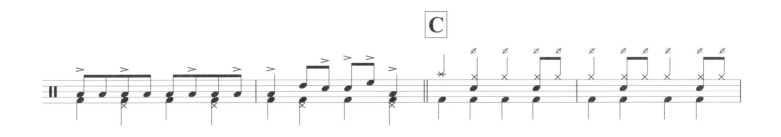

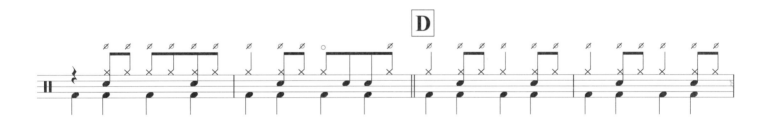

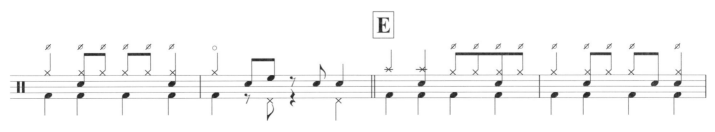

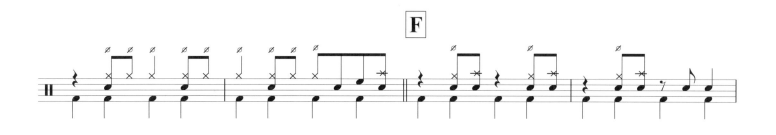

F

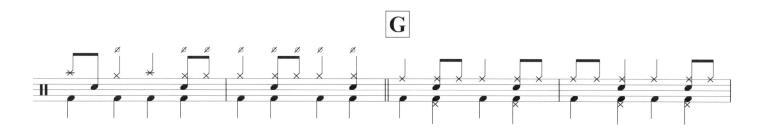

G

H

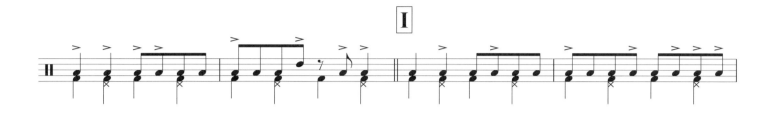

$\boxed{\text{I}}$

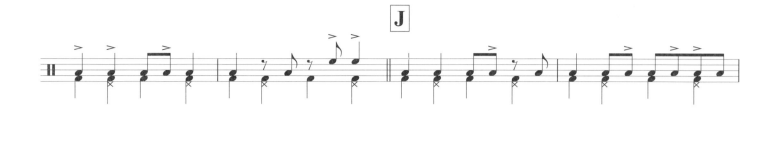

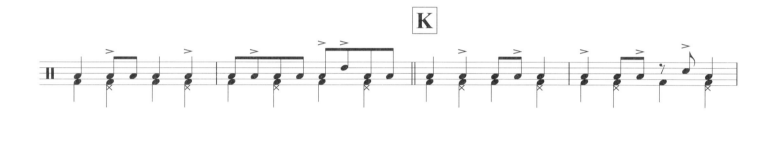

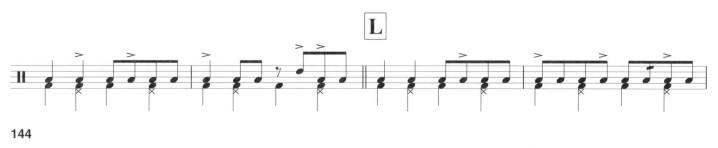

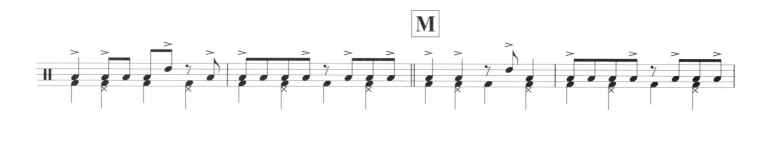

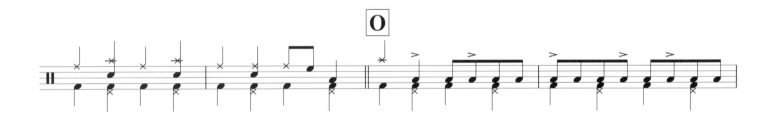

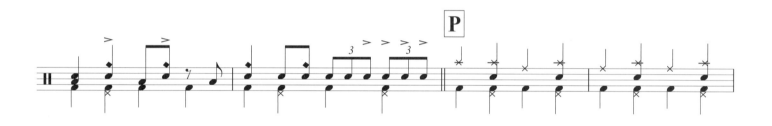

Smells Like Teen Spirit

Words and Music by Kurt Cobain, Krist Novoselic and Dave Grohl

Intro
Moderate Rock ♩ = 114

(Guitar)

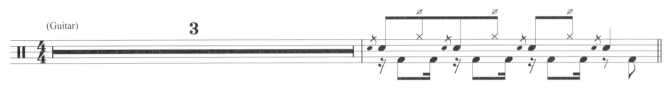

Play 7 times

Verse

Load up on guns...

Play 3 times

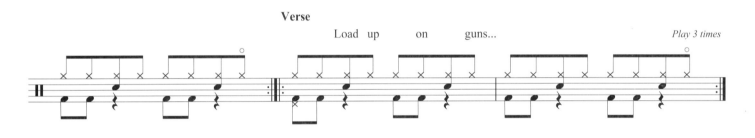

Pre-Chorus

Hel - lo, hel - lo...

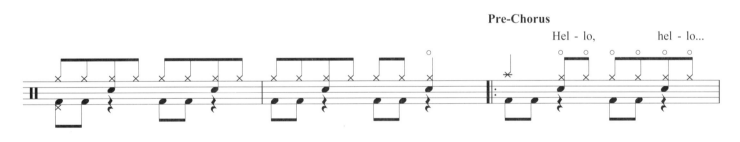

With the lights

Chorus

out   it's less dan - g'rous...

Bridge

yay,

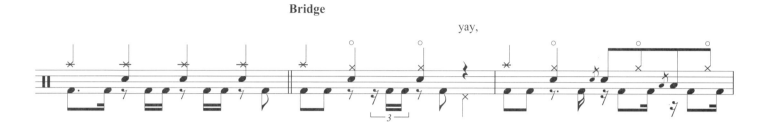

yay.

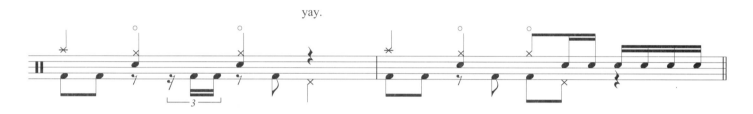

Verse

I'm worse   at   what...

Play 3 times

𝄋 **Pre-Chorus**

Hel - lo,   hel - lo...

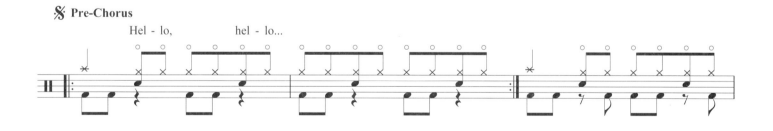

With the lights

Chorus

out   it's   less   dan - g'rous...

Play 4 times

To Coda ⊕

Bridge

Guitar Solo

Play 15 times

Verse

And   I   for - get...

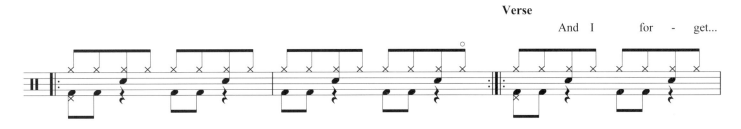

***D.S. al Coda*
*(take repeats)***

Play 3 times

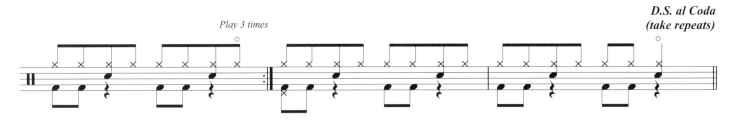

⊕ **Coda**

Play 7 times

Superstition

Words and Music by Stevie Wonder

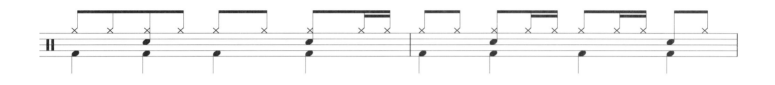

Ver - y   su - per - sti -

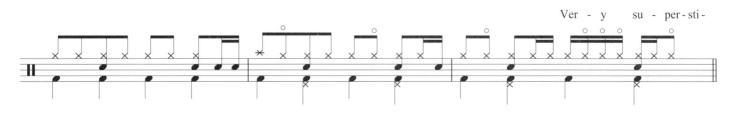

Verse

- tious,   wash your face and hands...

Interlude

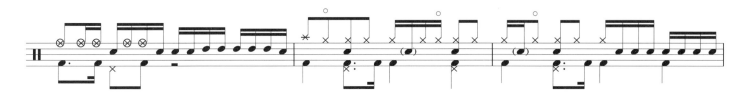

Ver - y su - per - sti -

Verse

- tious,   noth-ing more to say...

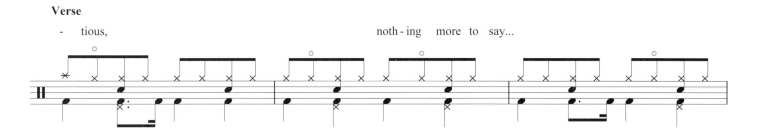

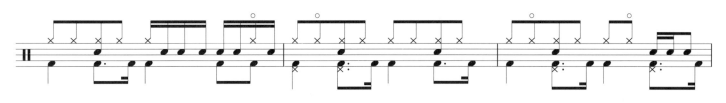

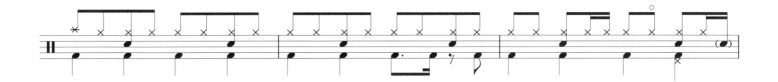

Outro

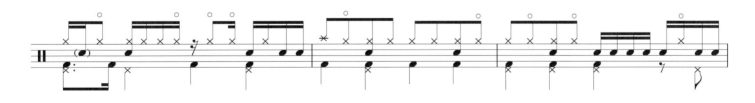

Fade out

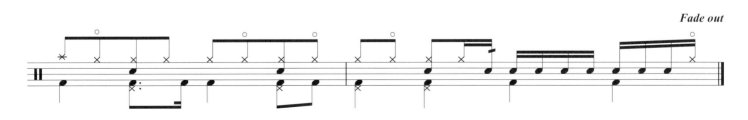

Sunday Bloody Sunday

Words and Music by U2

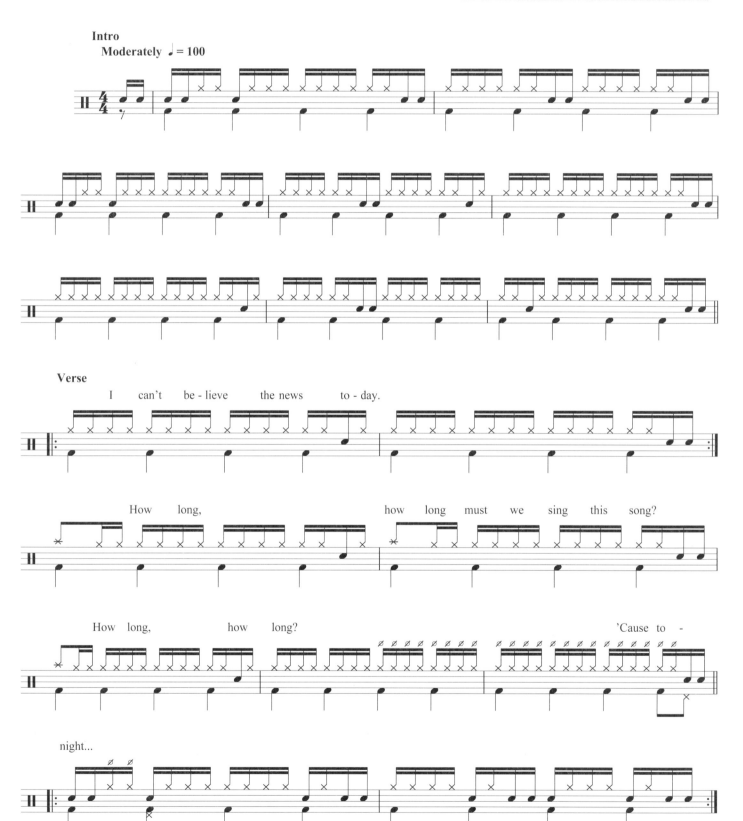

Verse

Bro - ken bot - tles un - der child - ren's feet.

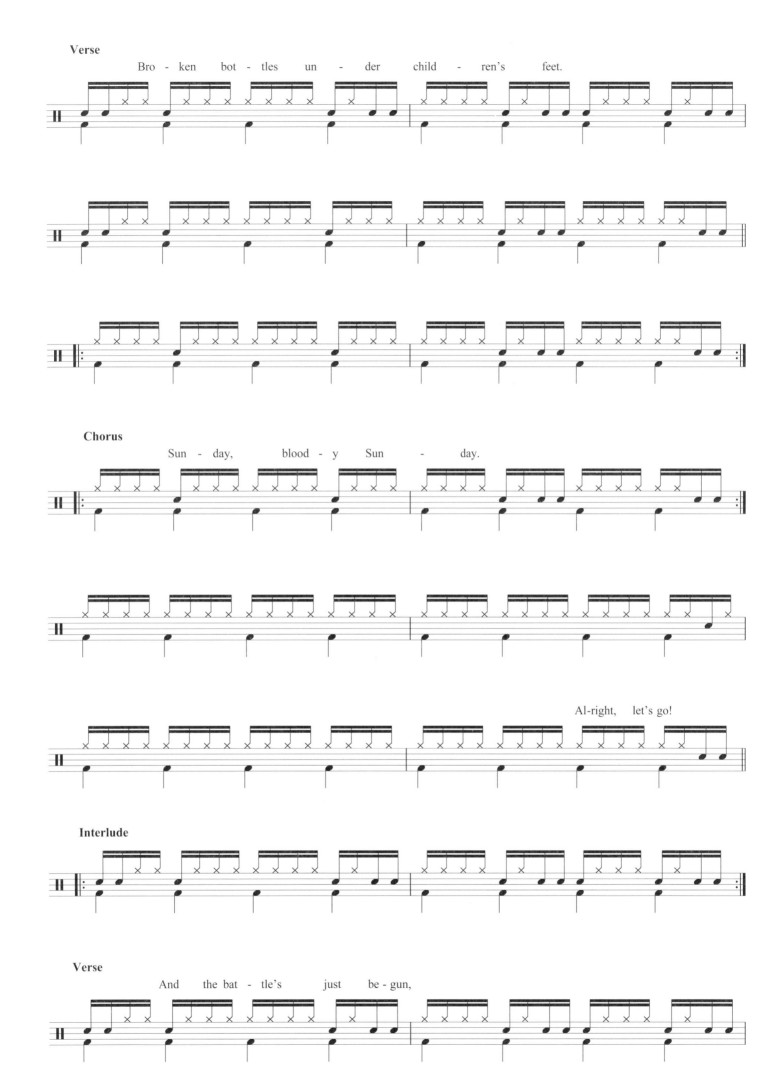

Chorus

Sun - day, blood - y Sun - day.

Al-right, let's go!

Interlude

Verse

And the bat - tle's just be - gun,

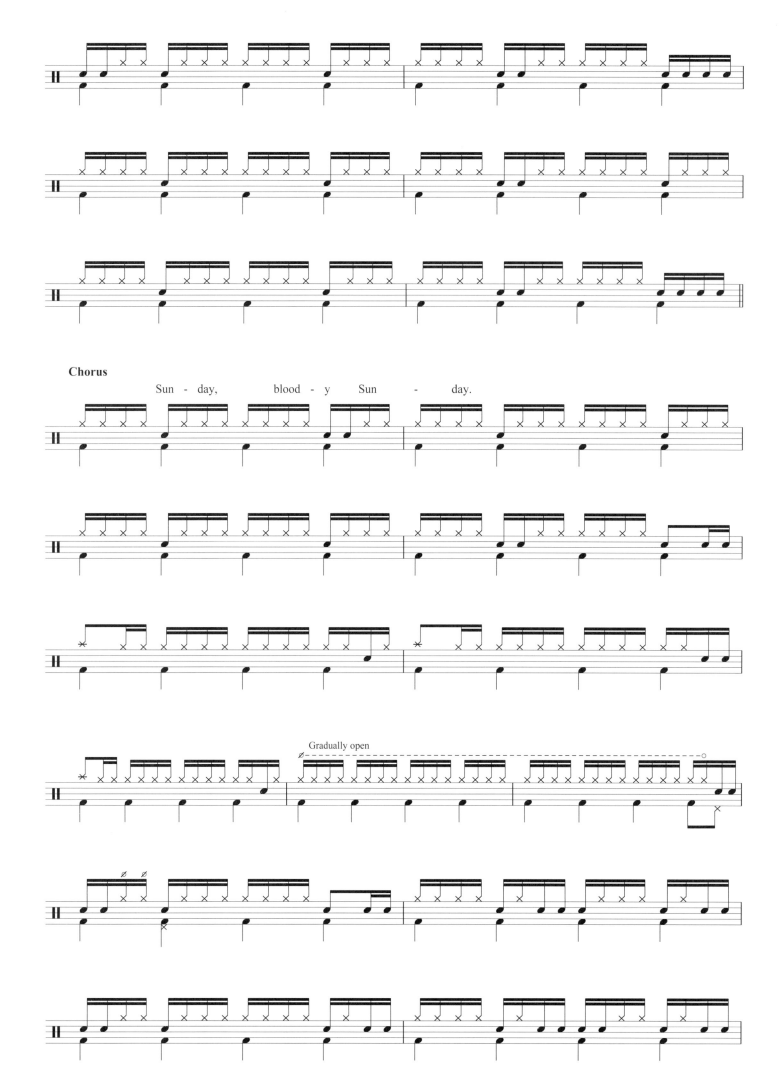

Chorus

Sun - day,   blood - y Sun - day.

Gradually open

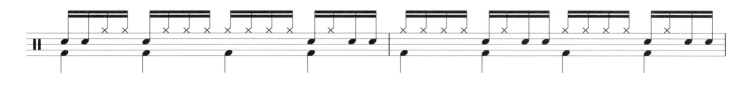

Guitar Solo

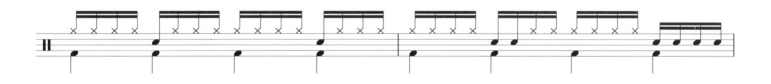

Bridge

Wipe the tears from

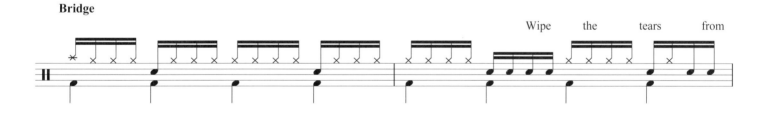

your eyes...

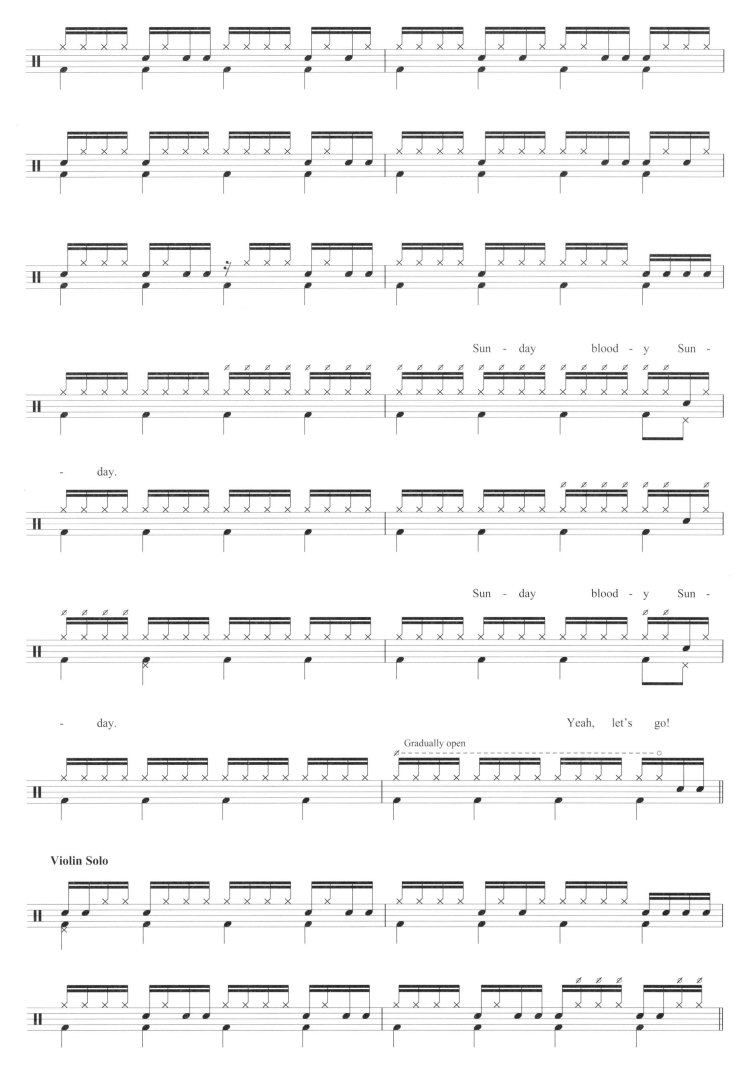

Sun - day blood - y Sun -

- day.

Sun - day blood - y Sun -

- day. Yeah, let's go!

Gradually open

Violin Solo

Outro-Verse

And it's true we are im - mune...

The Thrill Is Gone

Words and Music by Roy Hawkins and Rick Darnell

LEGEND

Drummer: Herbie Lovelle

Intro/Guitar Solo
Moderate Blues ♩ = 90

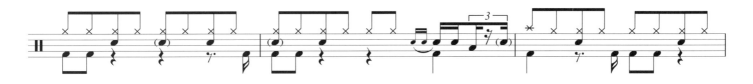

Verse

The thrill is gone,   the thrill is   gone...

Play 9 times

Verse

The thrill is gone...

Play 10 times

Guitar Solo

Play 9 times

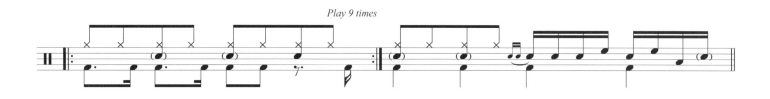

Verse

The thrill is gone...

Play 10 times

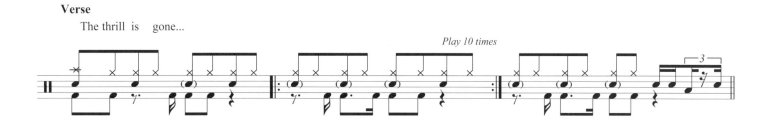

Verse

You know I'm free, free now...

Play 10 times

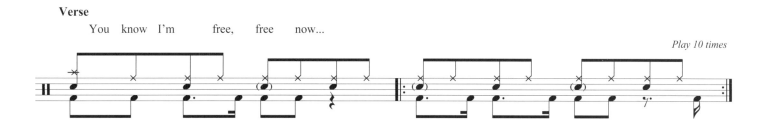

Outro-Guitar Solo

Repeat and fade

Under Pressure

Words and Music by Freddie Mercury, John Deacon,
Brian May, Roger Taylor and David Bowie

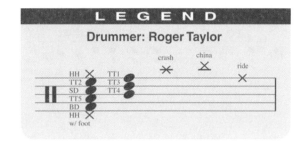

Intro
Moderately ♩ = 113

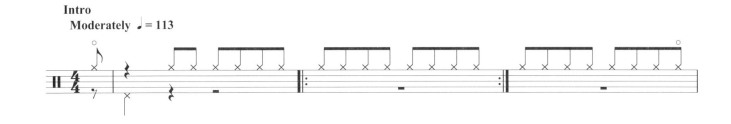

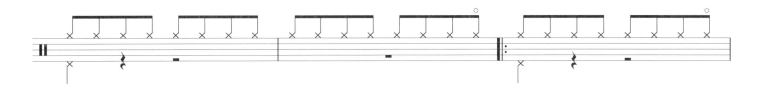

Play 3 times

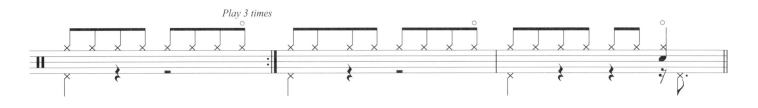

Verse

Pres - sure,　　　push - in' down　on　me...

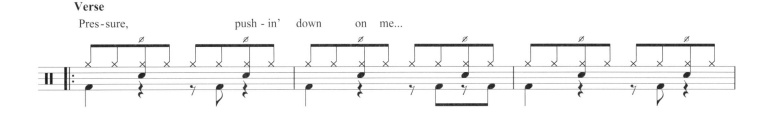

Chorus

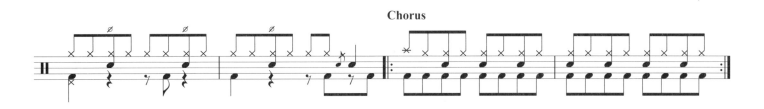

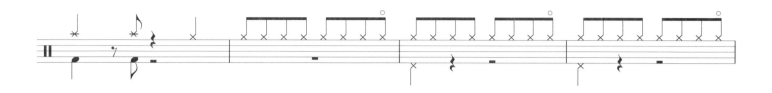

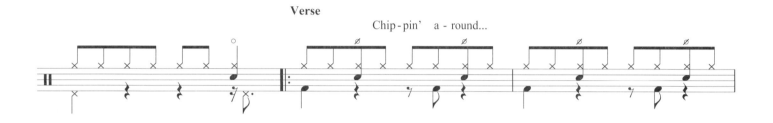

Verse

Chip-pin' a - round...

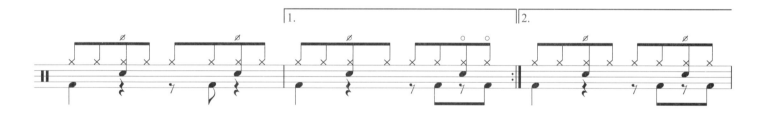

Chorus

Turned a -

Bridge

way   from it all   like a blind man...

Play 3 times

Can't   we

Verse

give our-selves   one more chance...

Chorus

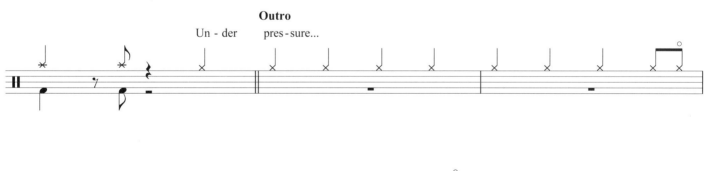

Outro

Un - der   pres - sure...

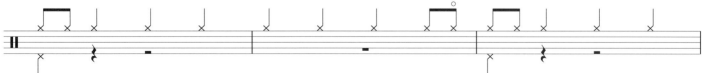

Repeat and fade

Uprising

Words and Music by Matthew Bellamy

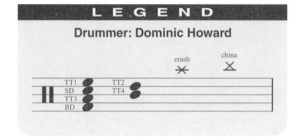

Interlude

Chorus

They

will   not...

Play 6 times

Play 6 times

Interlude

2

Verse

In - ter-chang-ing

mind con - trol...

1.   2.   3.

Interlude   **Chorus**

They

Play 3 times

3   3

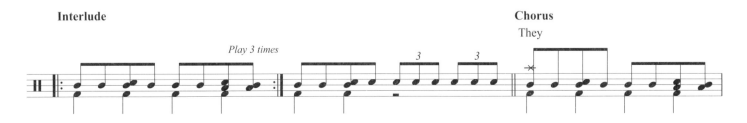

will   not   force   us...

Play 4 times

Interlude

Play 8 times

Chorus

They

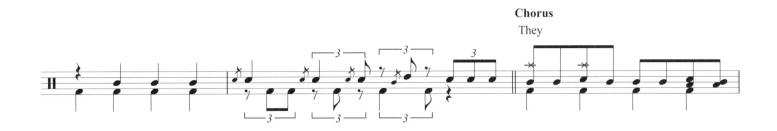

will   not   force   us...

Play 4 times   *Play 3 times*

Outro

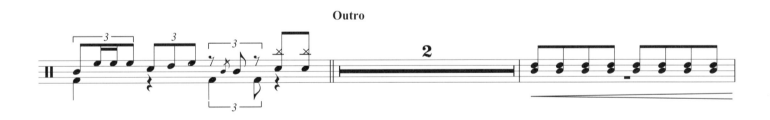

2

Play 3 times

Play 4 times

Walk This Way

Words and Music by Steven Tyler and Joe Perry

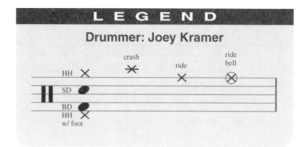

Intro
Moderate Rock ♩ = 120

Play 5 times

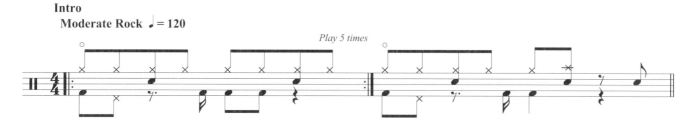

Verse

Back-stroke lov-er...

Play 6 times

𝄋 Interlude

Verse

See - saw swing-in'...

Play 6 times

To Coda ⊕

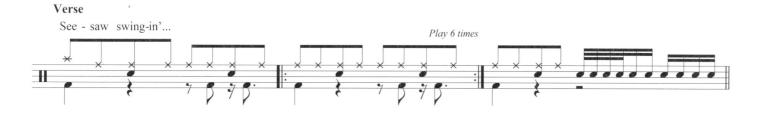

Chorus

Guitar Solo

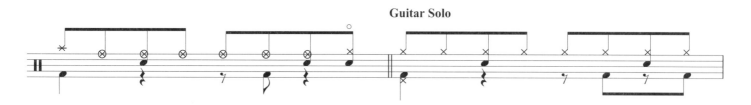

Interlude

Verse

School girl skin-ny...

D.S. al Coda
(take repeats)

Play 6 times

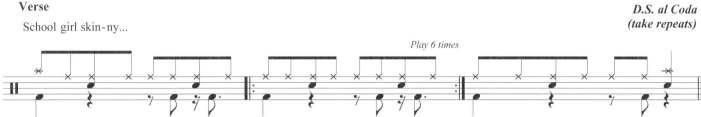

⊕ Coda

Guitar Solo

Play 7 times

Repeat and fade

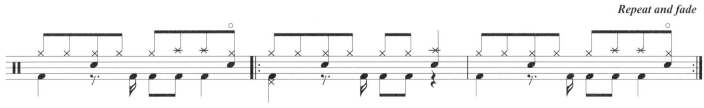

173

The Weight

By J.R. Robertson

Chorus

Take a load off, Fan - ny...

Verse

Go down, Miss Mo - ses...

Chorus

Take a load off, Fan - ny...

Verse

Cra - zy Ches - ter fol - lowed me...

Chorus

Take a load off, Fan - ny...

Verse

Catch   a can - non ball...

*Played as even sixteenth notes.

Chorus

Take a load off,   Fan - ny...

Willie and the Hand Jive

Words and Music by Johnny Otis

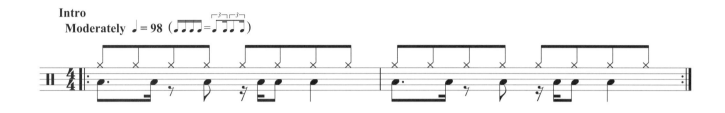

Intro
Moderately ♩ = 98

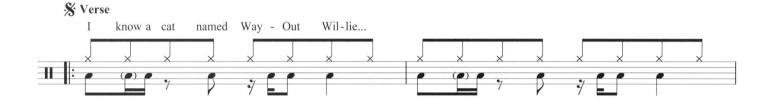

Verse

I know a cat named Way - Out Wil-lie...

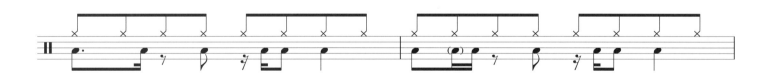

To Coda ⊕

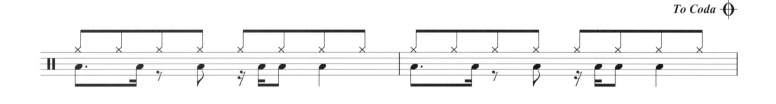

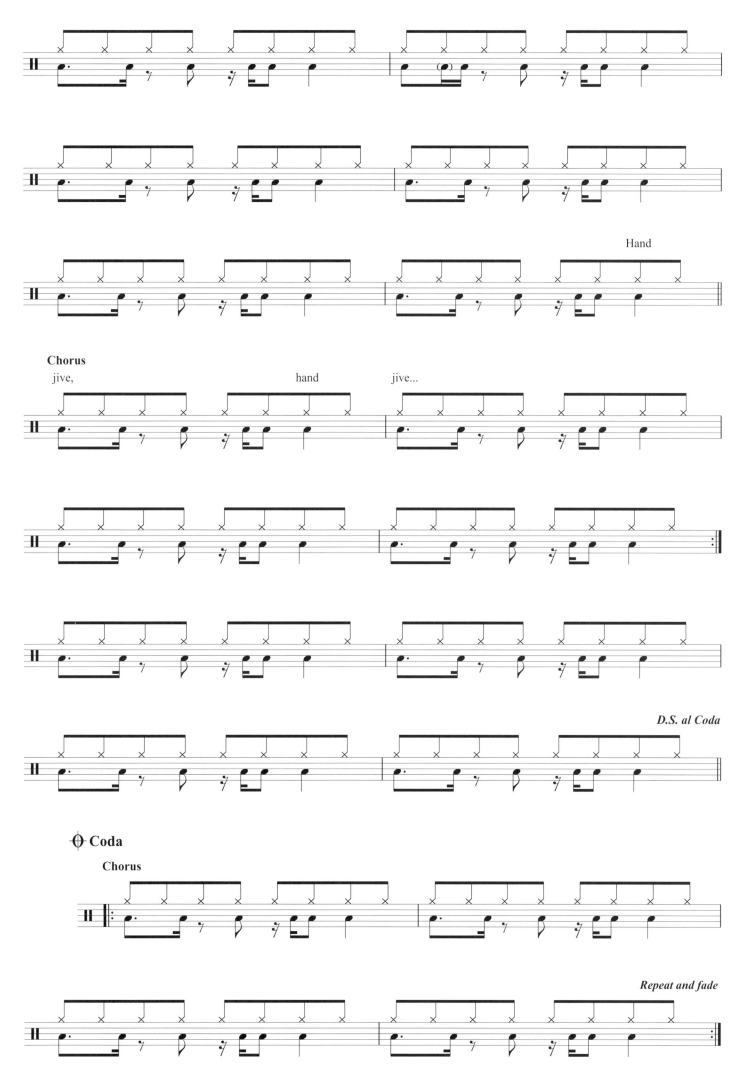

Hand

Chorus

jive,   hand   jive...

D.S. al Coda

Coda

Chorus

Repeat and fade

Wipe Out

By The Surfaris

A

Moderately fast ♩ = 162

B

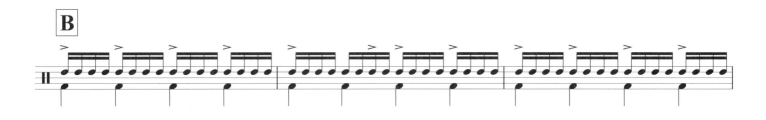

C

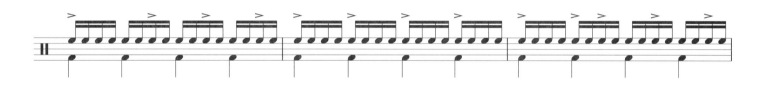

D

You Really Got Me

Words and Music by Ray Davies

LEGEND

Drummer: Mick Avory

Intro
Moderately ♩ = 138

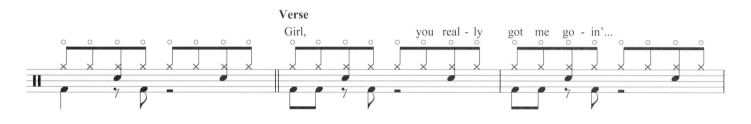

Verse

Girl,   you real - ly   got me go - in'...

Play 3 times

Verse

See,   don't ev - er   set me free...

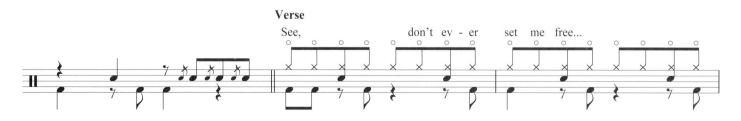

Guitar Solo

Play 3 times

Verse

See, don't ev - er

set me free...

DRUM TRANSCRIPTIONS
FROM HAL LEONARD

THE BEATLES DRUM COLLECTION

26 drum transcriptions of some of the Beatles' best, including: Back in the U.S.S.R. • Birthday • Can't Buy Me Love • Eight Days a Week • Help! • Helter Skelter • I Saw Her Standing There • Ob-La-Di, Ob-La-Da • Paperback Writer • Revolution • Sgt. Pepper's Lonely Hearts Club Band • Something • Twist and Shout • and more.

00690402 . . . . $19.99

BEST OF BLINK-182

Features Travis Barker's bashing beats from a baker's dozen of Blink's best. Songs: Adam's Song • Aliens Exist • All the Small Things • Anthem Part II • Dammit • Don't Leave Me • Dumpweed • First Date • Josie • Pathetic • The Rock Show • Stay Together for the Kids • What's My Age Again?

00690621 . . . . $22.99

DRUM CHART HITS

Authentic drum transcriptions of 30 pop and rock hits are including: Can't Stop the Feeling • Ex's & Oh's • Get Lucky • Moves like Jagger • Shake It Off • Thinking Out Loud • 24K Magic • Uptown Funk • and more.

00234062 . . . . $17.99

INCUBUS DRUM COLLECTION

Drum transcriptions for 13 of the biggest hits from this alt-metal band. Includes: Are You In? • Blood on the Ground • Circles • A Crow Left of the Murder • Drive • Megalomaniac • Nice to Know You • Pardon Me • Privilege • Stellar • Talk Shows on Mute • Wish You Were Here • Zee Deveel.

00690763 . . . . $17.95

BEST OF THE DAVE MATTHEWS BAND FOR DRUMS

Cherry Lane Music

Note-for-note transcriptions of Carter Beauford's great drum work: The Best of What's Around • Crash into Me • What Would You Say.

02500184 . . . . $19.95

DAVE MATTHEWS BAND – FAN FAVORITES FOR DRUMS

Cherry Lane Music

Exact drum transcriptions of every Carter Beauford beat from 10 of the most requested DMB hits: Crush • Dancing Nancies • Everyday • Grey Street • Jimi Thing • The Space Between • Tripping Billies • Two Step • Warehouse • Where Are You Going.

02500643 . . . . $19.95

METALLICA – …AND JUSTICE FOR ALL

Cherry Lane Music

Drum transcriptions to every song from Metallica's blockbuster album, plus complete drum setup diagrams, and background notes on Lars Ulrich's drumming style.

02503504 . . . . $19.99

METALLICA – BLACK

Cherry Lane Music

Matching folio to their critically acclaimed self-titled album. Includes: Enter Sandman * Sad But True * The Unforgiven * Don't Tread On Me * Of Wolf And Man * The God That Failed * Nothing Else Matters * and 5 more metal crunchers.

02503509 . . . . $22.99

METALLICA – MASTER OF PUPPETS

Cherry Lane Music

Matching folio to the best-selling album. Includes: Master Of Puppets • Battery • Leper Messiah • plus photos.

02503502 . . . . $19.99

METALLICA – RIDE THE LIGHTNING

Cherry Lane Music

Matching folio to Metallica's second album, including: Creeping Death • Fade To Black • and more.

02503507 . . . . $19.99

NIRVANA DRUM COLLECTION

Features transcriptions of Dave Grohl's actual drum tracks on 17 hits culled from four albums: *Bleach, Nevermind, Incesticide* and *In Utero*. Includes the songs: About a Girl • All Apologies • Blew • Come as You Are • Dumb • Heart Shaped Box • In Bloom • Lithium • (New Wave) Polly • Smells like Teen Spirit • and more. Also includes a drum notation legend.

00690316 . . . . $22.99

BEST OF RED HOT CHILI PEPPERS FOR DRUMS

Note-for-note drum transcriptions for every funky beat blasted by Chad Smith on 20 hits from *Mother's Milk* through *By the Way*! Includes: Aeroplane • Breaking the Girl • By the Way • Californication • Give It Away • Higher Ground • Knock Me Down • Me and My Friends • My Friends • Right on Time • Scar Tissue • Throw Away Your Television • True Men Don't Kill Coyotes • Under the Bridge • and more.

00690587 . . . . $24.99

RED HOT CHILI PEPPERS – GREATEST HITS

Essential for Peppers fans! Features Chad Smith's thunderous drumming transcribed note-for-note from their *Greatest Hits* album. 15 songs: Breaking the Girl • By the Way • Californication • Give It Away • Higher Ground • My Friends • Scar Tissue • Suck My Kiss • Under the Bridge • and more.

00690681 . . . . $22.99

RED HOT CHILI PEPPERS – I'M WITH YOU

Note-for-note drum transcriptions from the group's tenth album: The Adventures of Rain Dance Maggie • Annie Wants a Baby • Brendan's Death Song • Dance, Dance, Dance • Did I Let You Know • Ethiopia • Even You Brutus? • Factory of Faith • Goodbye Hooray • Happiness Loves Company • Look Around • Meet Me at the Corner • Monarchy of Roses • Police Station.

00691168 . . . . $22.99

RUSH – THE SPIRIT OF RADIO: GREATEST HITS 1974-1987

17 exact drum transcriptions from Neil Peart! Includes: Closer to the Heart • Fly by Night • Freewill • Limelight • Red Barchetta • Spirit of Radio • Subdivisions • Time Stand Still • Tom Sawyer • The Trees • Working Man • 2112 (I Overture & II Temples of Syrinx).

00323857 . . . . $22.99

HAL•LEONARD®

7777 W. BLUEMOUND RD. P.O. BOX 13819 MILWAUKEE, WI 53213

www.halleonard.com

0222
154

Prices, contents and availability subject to change without notice.

YOU CAN'T BEAT OUR DRUM BOOKS!

Bass Drum Control
Best Seller for More Than 50 Years!
by Colin Bailey
This perennial favorite among drummers helps players develop their bass drum technique and increase their flexibility through the mastery of exercises.
06620020 Book/Online Audio $17.99

The Complete Drumset Rudiments
by Peter Magadini
Use your imagination to incorporate these rudimental etudes into new patterns that you can apply to the drumset or tom toms as you develop your hand technique with the Snare Drum Rudiments, your hand and foot technique with the Drumset Rudiments and your polyrhythmic technique with the Polyrhythm Rudiments. Adopt them all into your own creative expressions based on ideas you come up with while practicing.
06620016 Book/CD Pack $14.95

Drum Aerobics
by Andy Ziker
A 52-week, one-exercise-per-day workout program for developing, improving, and maintaining drum technique. Players of all levels – beginners to advanced – will increase their speed, coordination, dexterity and accuracy. The online audio contains all 365 workout licks, plus play-along grooves in styles including rock, blues, jazz, heavy metal, reggae, funk, calypso, bossa nova, march, mambo, New Orleans 2nd Line, and lots more!
06620137 Book/Online Audio $19.99

Drumming the Easy Way!
The Beginner's Guide to Playing Drums for Students and Teachers
by Tom Hapke
Cherry Lane Music
Now with online audio! This book takes the beginning drummer through the paces – from reading simple exercises to playing great grooves and fills. Each lesson includes a preparatory exercise and a solo. Concepts and rhythms are introduced one at a time, so growth is natural and easy. Features large, clear musical print, intensive treatment of each individual drum figure, solos following each exercise to motivate students, and more!
02500876 Book/Online Audio...............................$19.99
02500191 Book...$14.99

The Drumset Musician – 2nd Edition
by Rod Morgenstein and Rick Mattingly
Containing hundreds of practical, usable beats and fills, *The Drumset Musician* teaches you how to apply a variety of patterns and grooves to the actual performance of songs. The accompanying online audio includes demos as well as 18 play-along tracks covering a wide range of rock, blues and pop styles, with detailed instructions on how to create exciting, solid drum parts.
00268369 Book/Online Audio...............................$19.99

Instant Guide to Drum Grooves
The Essential Reference for the Working Drummer
by Maria Martinez
Become a more versatile drumset player! From traditional Dixieland to cutting-edge hip-hop, *Instant Guide to Drum Grooves* is a handy source featuring 100 patterns that will prepare working drummers for the stylistic variety of modern gigs. The book includes essential beats and grooves in such styles as: jazz, shuffle, country, rock, funk, New Orleans, reggae, calypso, Brazilian and Latin.
06620056 Book/CD Pack $12.99

1001 Drum Grooves
The Complete Resource for Every Drummer
by Steve Mansfield
Cherry Lane Music
This book presents 1,001 drumset beats played in a variety of musical styles, past and present. It's ideal for beginners seeking a well-organized, easy-to-follow encyclopedia of drum grooves, as well as consummate professionals who want to bring their knowledge of various drum styles to new heights. Author Steve Mansfield presents: rock and funk grooves, blues and jazz grooves, ethnic grooves, Afro-Cuban and Caribbean grooves, and much more.
02500337 Book..$14.99

Polyrhythms – The Musician's Guide
by Peter Magadini
edited by Wanda Sykes
Peter Magadini's *Polyrhythms* is acclaimed the world over and has been hailed by *Modern Drummer* magazine as "by far the best book on the subject." Written for instrumentalists and vocalists alike, this book with online audio contains excellent solos and exercises that feature polyrhythmic concepts. Topics covered include: 6 over 4, 5 over 4, 7 over 4, 3 over 4, 11 over 4, and other rhythmic ratios; combining various polyrhythms; polyrhythmic time signatures; and much more. The audio includes demos of the exercises and is accessed online using the unique code in each book.
06620053 Book/Online Audio..............................$19.99

Joe Porcaro's Drumset Method – Groovin' with Rudiments
Patterns Applied to Rock, Jazz & Latin Drumset
by Joe Porcaro
Master teacher Joe Porcaro presents rudiments at the drumset in this sensational new edition of *Groovin' with Rudiments*. This book is chock full of exciting drum grooves, sticking patterns, fills, polyrhythmic adaptations, odd meters, and fantastic solo ideas in jazz, rock, and Latin feels. The online audio features 99 audio clip examples in many styles to round out this true collection of superb drumming material for every serious drumset performer.
06620129 Book/Online Audio $24.99

66 Drum Solos for the Modern Drummer
Rock • Funk • Blues • Fusion • Jazz
by Tom Hapke
Cherry Lane Music
66 Drum Solos for the Modern Drummer presents drum solos in all styles of music in an easy-to-read format. These solos are designed to help improve your technique, independence, improvisational skills, and reading ability on the drums and at the same time provide you with some cool licks that you can use right away in your own playing.
02500319 Book/Online Audio.................................$17.99

HAL•LEONARD®
www.halleonard.com

Prices, contents, and availability subject to change without notice.